S0-ABC-358

How to Train Your Boxer

liz palika

Photos by the author unless otherwise credited.

BOXER

The Publisher would like to thank the owners of dogs pictured in this book, including: Debbie Alport, Walter Amos, Ann and Steven Anderson, Lynn Baxter, Donna Butler, Dan Clipper, Michelle Deslauriers, Gerald and Tommie Eller, Arlene Freer, Dianna Helmke, Manuel Izquierdo, Thelma Jacobson, Pat Mullen, Randy Ortlieb, Richard Tomaca, Richard Tomita, and Virginia Zurflieh

Distributed in the UNITED STATES to the Pet Trade by T.F.H. Publications, Inc., 1 TFH Plaza, Neptune City, NJ 07753; on the Internet at www.tfh.com; in CANADA by Rolf C. Hagen Inc., 3225 Sartelon St., Montreal, Quebec H4R 1E8; Pet Trade by H & L Pet Supplies Inc., 27 Kingston Crescent, Kitchener, Ontario N2B 2T6; in ENGLAND by T.F.H. Publications, PO Box 74, Havant PO9 5TT; in AUSTRALIA AND THE SOUTH PACIFIC by T.F.H. (Australia), Pty. Ltd., Box 149, Brookvale 2100 N.S.W., Australia; in NEW ZEALAND by Brooklands Aquarium Ltd., 5 McGiven Drive, New Plymouth, RD1 New Zealand; in SOUTH AFRICA by Rolf C. Hagen S.A. (PTY.) LTD., P.O. Box 201199, Durban North 4016, South Africa; in JAPAN by T.F.H. Publications, Japan—Jiro Tsuda, 10-12-3 Ohjidai, Sakura, Chiba 285, Japan. Published by T.F.H. Publications, Inc.

MANUFACTURED IN THE
UNITED STATES OF AMERICA
BY T.F.H. PUBLICATIONS, INC.

contents

INTRODUCTION

Boxers are muscular, solidly built working dogs. Aside from being loyal protectors, their gentle and playful demeanor makes them wonderful companions. This is Pete, owned by Thelma Jacobson.

Thelma Jacobson's Boxer, Pete, is a lovely chestnut-red color, with a black muzzle and white feet. He is a solid, muscular dog, but gentle as a lamb—unless you happen to get in his way as he's chasing after a tennis ball! Then watch out! Thelma said of her 18-month-old dog, "He's still very much a puppy right now. He still has a one-track mind and, when he's concentrating on his ball, that's *all* he's thinking about!"

Thelma isn't making excuses for Pete; she's had Boxers before and knows they take awhile to mature. With all her dogs, Pete included, she emphasizes good manners and obedience training so that when they grow up, they will have good social skills and will be wonderful companions. Meanwhile, she maintains her patience with Pete as he continues to show his immaturity and ongoing puppyhood.

Potential Boxer owners need to understand the breed before adding one to the family. Pete's owner knew that Boxers are slow to mature and can act like puppies for a couple of years. Potential owners need to understand, too, that Boxers are solid, muscular dogs; this is not a lightweight breed!

Boxers need daily exercise and regular training sessions. They need a job to do, even if it's as easy as bringing in the morning newspaper.

If you can meet the expectations of a Boxer and go into the relationship understanding where this breed came from and its needs today, then go ahead and get a Boxer. You will have a wonderful, loyal friend, companion, and protector.

Learning good manners and obedience skills can help ensure that your Boxer will be a treasured member of the family for years to come.

1 SELECTING the Right Dog for You

WHAT ARE BOXERS?

In the Beginning

Although Boxers, as we know them, originated from planned breedings in Germany in the last 100 years, ancestors of today's Boxers can be traced back for centuries. Alexander the Great had some huge mastiff-type dogs that share the same wide smile that Boxers have. The Romans also had large, strong, wide-mouthed dogs called Britannic Mastiffs. These two types of dog interbred and eventually shared the name Molossian Hounds (even though they were not what we today consider hounds).

Boxer history also claims the breed is related to ancient Tibetan fighting dogs, central European Bullenbeisser (bull-baiter) dogs, and dogs used to hunt stag in Spain. Early 16th and 17th century tapestries depict Spanish dogs taking part in stag and boar hunts. These dogs share

Originating in Germany, the Boxer is a breed known for its intelligence, fearlessness, and strength combined with style.

Photo by Isabelle Francais

The Boxer is named for his style of playing and fighting, which always begins with the front paws, much like a human boxer using his fists.

enough characteristics with today's Boxers that they appear to be ancestors or share a common ancestry.

The Boxer we know today came into being in Germany in the late 1800s. Keeping the breed's old qualities, including the wide mouth, the breed became known for its intelligence, fearlessness, and strength. In fact, the Boxer was so widely appreciated, it was the first breed selected for police training in Germany.

The Boxer Today

Today's Boxer is a medium-sized dog, 22 to 25 in. tall at the shoulder, with weight appropriate to height. Having a relatively short back, Boxers give the impression of standing square. Developed to be a working dog, the Boxer's physical presence gives the impression of power, agility, and

THE BOXER NAME

If Germany had so much influence on the breed, why does it bear an obviously English name? *The Complete Dog Book*, by the American Kennel Club (AKC), says that the breed is named for its style of playing and fighting, which always begins with the front paws, much like a human boxer using his fists.

strength combined with style.

The Boxer has a short, slick coat that lies close to the body. Colors range from a light tan to a dark red mahogany. Brindle, darker stripes (dark brown or black) on a fawn background, is also acceptable. White markings are acceptable, and may include white paws or legs, a white blaze up the face, and white on the front of the chest. The muzzle is usually black, but may have some white around the front of it.

The Boxer's head is one of his most unique attributes. The muzzle should be blunt and wide, with the lower jaw undershot, creating the typical Boxer smile. The head should be strong, with the face conveying character and expression. The eyes should be dark brown, intelligent, and alert. The ears are set up high on the sides of the head. Traditionally, the ears have been cropped, but more often breeders and owners are leaving the ears natural. The tail is almost always docked.

Temperament

Boxers are courageous, self-confident, calm, even-tempered dogs. They are affectionate with their people, bonding strongly to everyone in the family, but cautious and

An elegant, medium-sized dog, the Boxer has a short, slick coat that lies close to the body in colors ranging from light tan to dark red mahogany.

Photo by Isabelle Francais

reserved with strangers. Boxers need to have plenty of time with their owners: time to play and exercise, time to learn obedience skills and social rules, and time to simply be quiet. This desire to be with their people affects all aspects of the Boxer's life.

Benjamin L. Hart, DVM, and Lynette A. Hart, authors of *The Perfect Puppy*, said of the Boxer temperament, "The behavioral profile of the Boxer is moderate in all its traits—not too reactive (it has been used as a guide dog), not too sluggish, not terribly aggressive—but no pushover, either." They continue by warning prospective owners that Boxers are very territorial and will protect what they consider to be their property.

Because Boxers bond strongly with everyone in the family, your companionship is necessary for their happiness and well-being. This desire to be with people affects all aspects of the Boxer's life.

A Boxer is not a good dog to leave alone in the backyard all day. Left alone too much, they may become escape artists, trying desperately to escape from the yard. Boxers left alone too often may also become depressed, despondent, morose, and unhappy.

Bred to be working dogs, Boxers make good watchdogs. Distrustful of strangers, the Boxer will pay close attention to the mail carrier, the parcel delivery man, and neighborhood children. Boxers are usually not problem barkers and will not bark as much as other breeds might when trespassers come to the door; however, that doesn't mean the Boxer isn't paying attention—he is! He's just doing so quietly.

Boxers are excellent working dogs and take their jobs seriously, no matter what they might be. Boxers have been used as guard dogs, guide dogs, service dogs, therapy dogs, search and rescue dogs, and more.

Don't let this working heritage fool you, though. As their owners will readily tell you, Boxers are clowns and love to play. Puppies will play with anything—chasing balls, butterflies, and even an airplane high above. Even mature adults retain their sense of fun and will turn into clowns when given any excuse to do so.

IS A BOXER THE RIGHT DOG FOR YOU?

Evaluating Your Personality and Lifestyle

The decision to add a dog to your family is not a decision that should be taken lightly. This is a 14- to 15-year commitment, and Boxers are intelligent, affectionate dogs with some specific needs.

Do you work long hours, come home tired, and just want to relax, spending the evening reading or watching television? If you do, an older, mature Boxer would be a better choice for you than a puppy or young dog.

Do you come home tired, but enjoy doing things outside, like riding a bicycle? If so, an adult dog might be suited to your lifestyle. Do you work at home, have short work hours, or enjoy hobbies? If so, a puppy or an active young dog should please you.

Don't let their working heritage fool you—Boxers are affectionate with their people and love to play. Even mature adults will turn into clowns when given any excuse to do so.

Photo by Tara Darling

Photo by Isabelle Francais

Before deciding to bring a Boxer puppy into your home, it is important to do your homework and learn as much as you can about the breed.

Being the center of a dog's world can be thrilling to some people and overwhelming to others. If you don't like being followed, watched, or touched, don't get a Boxer. A Boxer will want to be close to you and follow you from room to room. When you sit down, he will be lying at your feet. When you leave the house, the Boxer will want to go with you. Obviously, having a dog with you 24 hours a day is impossible for most people; however, if you want a Boxer, you will need to be able to provide as much companionship as possible.

Before thinking about getting a Boxer, look at your life realistically. A Boxer could be a wonderful companion for many, but is not the right breed for everyone. A Boxer should not be left alone for many hours a day or owned by a person that doesn't appreciate a dog's closeness. Nor should a Boxer be owned by someone who doesn't enjoy activity, because Boxers do.

The Boxer's Needs

All dogs have some specific needs, so before you add a dog

to your family, think about the following things. It could mean the difference between having a successful relationship with a dog or giving the dog up later.

First, companionship is very important. As mentioned earlier, Boxers need to spend time with their people. You must also be willing to take the time to train your dog. Being a very intelligent dog, if you don't train your Boxer, he will train you.

You will need to have a securely fenced yard or dog run. As a protective, working dog, a Boxer may try to get out of the backyard to protect the front yard and, if the yard isn't securely fenced, there could be problems. In addition, your Boxer may try to escape from the yard to try to find you. A large, securely fenced yard is wonderful, but even a dog run (no smaller than 6 feet by 30 feet) is acceptable, as long as the dog gets plenty of time out of the run when you're at home.

You must also have some means of exercising your Boxer. For example, if you like to jog, that's fine, but if you are not a jogger you will need to think of some other way of exercising your dog. Perhaps you can teach the dog to run next to your bicycle, or you can take the dog swimming. A healthy, young Boxer needs good, vigorous exercise on a daily basis.

Dog ownership is a long-term commitment, so be sure your lifestyle will permit you to fulfill your Boxer's need for vigorous exercise, training, and daily companionship. If you do not appreciate a dog's closeness or do not like activity—don't get a Boxer!

Photo by Isabelle Francais

SELECTING THE RIGHT DOG

Male or Female?

There are a lot of myths concerning the personality traits of both males and females. Ultimately, each dog will have an individual personality, regardless of gender. Spayed bitches (females) and neutered dogs (males) are usually a little calmer than those that are not. Spaying and neutering removes sexual hormones and, as a result, also removes the sexual tension that can accompany those hormones. To be a good pet and companion, your Boxer doesn't need those hormones anyway.

Boxers do vary in size by sex and this may affect your choice. A male Boxer that stands 25 in. tall at the shoulder could weigh 75 pounds. That's a big dog. Females are generally shorter and smaller.

Male Boxers tend to be a little more protective and territorial than females, but females tend to accept training better than males. However, both of these statements are generalizations as individual dogs may vary from these tendencies.

Photo by Isabelle Francais

Although every dog has an individual personality regardless of gender, male Boxers tend to be more protective and territorial than females, but females accept training better.

What Age?

Puppies are adorable, especially Boxer puppies, with their round tummies, big heads, and huge paws. However, when you add a puppy to your family, it's just like adding a baby to the family. Puppies, like babies, need to eat often, sleep a lot, relieve themselves frequently, and demand a lot of your time and attention.

As your puppy matures, he will become an integral part of your family, and by the time your Boxer is fully grown (in two to two-and-a-half years), he will have become a good friend. In the meantime, raising a puppy is a lot of work and, for many, adding a puppy to their life may not be the best choice. But that doesn't mean they can't have a dog. There are many adult Boxers that need good homes, and one of these dogs could be just the answer for people who do not have the time or patience to spend with a young puppy.

There are, unfortunately, some negative factors in adopting an adult dog. The process can be compared to buying a used car—sometimes you get a gem; sometimes you get a lemon! Not knowing how the dog has been treated prior to your ownership may affect his future behavior. Often, too, the dog's past health (and health care) is unknown.

Newly adopted dogs require time to settle into their new homes and to make emotional and physical adjustments. Because Boxers are so attached to their people, changing homes can be very traumatic. A newly adopted Boxer may become very clingy and show signs of separation anxiety whenever he is left alone. Usually, these behaviors will decrease as the dog settles into the new home, bonds with his new owners, and begins to feel more comfortable.

An adult Boxer may be just the answer for people who do not have the patience or time to spend housebreaking and training a young puppy.

Photo by Isabelle Francais

Finding an Adult Dog

If you have decided that an adult Boxer would be a better choice for you than a puppy, there are a few different places you can look for your new companion. Check your local shelter or humane society. Boxers are given up for a variety of reasons; perhaps an owner passed away or was transferred overseas, or perhaps the owner didn't realize what a Boxer was like and gave up after a few months. Whatever the reason, people will often bring these dogs to a local shelter.

Photo by Vince Serbin

If you are considering adoption, keep in mind that newly adopted dogs will require time to settle into their new homes and to make emotional and physical adjustments.

Evaluating an Adult Dog

Once you have found an adult Boxer, how do you decide if this is the right dog for you? First, do you like this dog? Your feelings for the animal are certainly going to play a big part in your relationship with him, so if you don't feel something right away, you should probably keep looking. However, don't say "yes" to this dog just because you do like him; there is more to making a selection than that.

For instance, do you know why this dog was given up by his owner? Sometimes the dog was given up through no fault of his own; however, if the owner gave him up because of behavior problems, you need to know that. Has the dog had any obedience training? Is he housetrained? These are important issues because even if you are willing to do some training, housetraining a previously untrained adult Boxer can be quite an undertaking.

What is the dog's personality like? Boxers are usually happy dogs, with a touch of the clown visible in their eyes and smile. However, a great many things can affect a

Photo by Isabelle Francais

There are many places you can look for a canine companion—check your local humane society or breed club-sponsored rescue groups, which prescreen dogs taken in for adoption.

dog's personality, including poor breeding practices, lack of socialization as a puppy, and more. When you whistle or speak to the dog, what does he do? Does he look at you and wag the stub of his tail? Great! If he looks sideways at you, slinks, or bares his throat, be careful. This dog is worried or scared, and a fearful dog may bite. Be careful, too, if the dog stands on his tiptoes and stares you in the eye. This is a challenging position and the dog could become potentially aggressive.

Ideally, you want a dog that is happy to see you without showing any worry, fearfulness, or aggression. You want a dog that is housetrained and, hopefully, has had some basic training. Make sure the dog's behavior problems are ones that you can live with now and are willing to work on in the future.

Finding a Puppy

If you have the time, patience, and resources to raise a puppy, you will want to find a reputable breeder. Breeder referrals can come from many sources. Other owners can refer you to their

RESCUE GROUPS

Many breed clubs sponsor or run breed rescue groups. Rescue groups screen the dogs taken in for adoption, which can be very beneficial. The dogs will have been checked by an expert in the breed for personality flaws (such as aggressiveness) and for obedience skills (or lack thereof). They are then vaccinated and spayed or neutered. This initial screening can serve as a prescreening process for you, taking some of the uncertainty out of the adoption process. To find a local Boxer rescue group in your area, check with your local shelter or humane society.

breeder. Your veterinarian might have a Boxer breeder as a client. Many national dog magazines have advertisements for breeders. You may also want to attend a dog show in your community and get information from the people there.

Once you locate several breeders, make an appointment to meet with them and ask questions. Ask if they are active in dog shows and dog sports. If the breeders show their dogs in conformation dog shows, their animals are probably good examples of the breed. If they participate in obedience competitions, their dogs are trainable. However, if they compete in Schutzhund (German protection competition) their dogs might be a little too reactive to make good family pets.

If breeders belong to national and local Boxer clubs, they are more likely to be up-to-date on news within the breed. Breed club newsletters and magazines usually publish articles concerning the breed's health and well-being.

Ask breeders what health problems they have seen in their dogs. If the breeder says none, be skeptical. A breed or line with no health problems at all is rare. Boxers can have a number of problems, including hip dysplasia, bloat, and allergies, to name just a few. Breeders should be honest with you about potential health threats and what they are doing to try to prevent future problems.

Photo by Isabelle Francais

To help ensure a successful relationship with your Boxer, choose a dog whose personality will suit yours. For example, if you are outgoing and extroverted, an active playful dog is a good match, whereas a quiet, submissive dog would do well with a quiet person or less active retiree.

Ask breeders to provide you with a list of references. Keep in mind that breeders will give you a list of people they know are happy with their dogs, but that's okay. You can still ask

Photo by Isabelle Francais

Attending a dog show in your area is a good way to get information and breeder referrals from Boxer experts and owners.

owners about their experiences. Did the breeder work well with them? Did she provide all the promised paperwork? Would they buy a puppy from the breeder again?

Caring breeders will ask you as many questions as you ask them. They want to know if you are the right person for one of their puppies. Don't get defensive—they are trying to do the right thing. Instead, answer the questions honestly.

Reputable breeders are up-to-date on health-related issues, which helps them to produce the best quality puppies.

Photo by Isabelle Francais

If, by some chance, a breeder says her dogs are not right for you, listen to her, because she knows her dogs better than you do.

Photo by Isabelle Francais

The Boxer puppy you choose should be bright-eyed, healthy, responsive, and curious about the world around him.

Evaluating a Puppy

Each puppy has his own personality and finding the right personality to match with yours is sometimes a challenge. For example, if you are outgoing, extroverted, and active, a quiet, withdrawn, submissive puppy would not fit well into your household and lifestyle. You will need a puppy more like you. On the other hand, that quiet puppy might do very well with a quiet person or a less active retiree.

When you go look at a puppy or a litter of puppies, there are several things you can do with the puppy to help evaluate his personality. First, with the puppy away from his mother or littermates, place him on the ground and walk a few steps away. Squat down and call the puppy to you. An outgoing, extroverted puppy will come happily and try to climb into your lap. If you stand up and walk away, the extrovert will follow you, trying to get underfoot. If you throw a piece of crumpled paper a few feet away, he will dash after it quickly. This Boxer would do well with an owner who is just as much of an extrovert as he is. He will need training to teach him self-control, lots of exercise, and a job to occupy his bright mind.

A quiet, submissive puppy will come to you when you call, but may do a belly crawl or roll over and bare his belly. When you get up to walk away, he will watch you but may be hesitant to follow you. If you toss the paper, he may go after it but be hesitant to bring it back to you. This puppy will need a quiet owner, gentle handling, and positive training.

These two puppies

demonstrate extremes in Boxer temperaments, and most Boxers are somewhere in between these two personality types. Try to find a puppy with a personality that will suit yours. Don't get an active puppy in the hope of making yourself more active if by nature you are a couch potato. It won't work, and the active puppy will drive you nuts! Nor should you get a puppy of a certain personality type in the hope of changing him; that won't work either. Find the puppy that is right for you.

BE CAREFUL!

Adding a Boxer to your family should be a time of anticipation and excitement, but to make it work requires thought, research, and preparation. Without preparation, the entire process could easily become a nightmare! Unfortunately, horror stories abound of puppies bought or adopted on impulse and given up later because the relationship didn't work. Hopefully, a Boxer will be a friend and companion for the next 14 years, so first, make sure a Boxer is the right breed for you, and second, choose the right dog with care.

Watching the way a Boxer puppy behaves with his littermates will tell you a lot about his temperament.

Photo by Isabelle Francais

2 Canine DEVELOPMENT Stages

Experts now feel that dogs were first domesticated as long as 135,000 years ago. In spite of this long, shared history, the bond that we have with dogs must be renewed with each puppy. The bond itself is not hereditary, although the tendency to bond is. This relationship is what makes owning a dog so special, but it doesn't happen automatically. To understand when and how this bond develops, it's important to understand that your Boxer is a dog—not a person in a fuzzy dog suit.

FAMILIES AND PACKS

Most researchers agree that the ancestors of today's dogs were wolves. However, they disagree on what wolves those ancestors were; they were either ancestors of today's grey wolves, or perhaps a species of wolf that is now extinct. In any event, wolves

Dogs, like their ancestors the wolves, are social creatures that live in extended families or "packs." To nurture the bond between you and your Boxer, establish yourself as the pack leader from the beginning of your relationship.

Photo by Isabelle Francais

Extremely loyal and inordinately fond of "kissing," Boxers thrive on pleasing their owners and will develop strong protective instincts as they mature.

are social creatures that live in an extended family pack. The pack might consist of a dominant (alpha) male and a dominant (alpha) female, and these two are usually the only two that breed. There will also be subordinate males and females, juveniles, and puppies. This is a very harmonious group that hunts together, plays together, defends its territory against intruders, and cares for each other. The only discord occurs when there is a change in the pack order. If one of the leaders becomes disabled, if an adult leaves the pack, or if a subordinate adult tries to assume dominance, there may be some jockeying to fill that position.

Many experts feel domesticated dogs adapt so well to our lifestyle because we, too, live in groups. Although we call them families instead of packs, they are still social groups. However, the comparison isn't really accurate; our families are much more chaotic than the average wolf pack. We are terribly inconsistent with our social rules and rules of behavior. (For example, we let our Boxer jump up and paw us when we're in grubby clothes and yell at him when he jumps up on our good

For the first few weeks of life, a Boxer puppy's mother is his key to survival and his source of food, warmth, and security.

Photo by Isabelle Francais

clothes!) To the dog, our communication skills are also confusing; our voice says one thing, while our body language says something else. To our dogs, we are very complex, confusing creatures. We can say that both dogs and humans live in social groups, and we can use that comparison to understand a little more about our dogs. However, we must also understand that our families are very different from a wolf pack.

FROM BIRTH TO FOUR WEEKS OF AGE

For the first three weeks of life, the family and the pack are unimportant as far as the baby Boxer is concerned. The only one of any significance is his mother. She is the key to his survival and the source of food, warmth, and security.

At four weeks of age, the baby Boxer's needs are still being met by his mother, but his littermates are becoming more important. His brothers and sisters provide warmth and security when their mother leaves the nest. His curiosity is developing and he will climb on and over his littermates, learning their scent and feel. During this period, he will learn to use his sense of hearing to follow

It is important to provide your dog with a nutritionally fortified diet geared toward his stage of life. Look for foods that are naturally preserved, contain no by-products, and are 100% guaranteed. Photo courtesy of Midwestern Pet Foods, Inc.

Photo by Isabelle Francais

A Boxer puppy should never be taken from his mother too soon—the discipline he receives from her during early stages of development will teach the pup to accept correction, training, and affection as he grows into adulthood.

sounds and his sense of vision to follow moving objects.

His mom will also start disciplining the puppies—very gently, of course—and this early discipline is vitally important to the puppies' future acceptance of discipline and training.

The breeder should be working with the puppies now to get them used to gentle handling. At this age, puppies can learn the difference between their mother's touch and gentle handling from people.

WEEKS FIVE THROUGH SEVEN

The young Boxer goes through some tremendous

LET THE MOTHER DOG CORRECT

Some inexperienced breeders will stop the mother dog from correcting her puppies, perhaps thinking that she is impatient, tired, or a poor mother. When the mother dog is not allowed to correct the puppies naturally, they do not learn how to accept discipline and later have a hard time when their new owner tries to establish some rules. Orphaned puppies raised by people suffer from the same problems. The mother dog knows instinctively what to do for her babies, and sometimes a correction—a low growl, a bark, or a snap of the teeth—is exactly what is needed.

changes between five and seven weeks of age. He is learning to recognize people and is starting to respond to individual voices. Playing more with his littermates, wrestling, and scuffling will teach each puppy how to get along, how to play, when the play is too rough, when to be submissive, and what to take seriously. His mother's discipline at this stage of development teaches the puppy to accept corrections, training, and affection.

The puppies should never be taken from their mother at this stage of development. Puppies taken away now and sent to new homes may have lasting behavior problems. They often have difficulty dealing with other dogs, may have trouble accepting rules and discipline, and may become excessively shy, aggressive, or fearful.

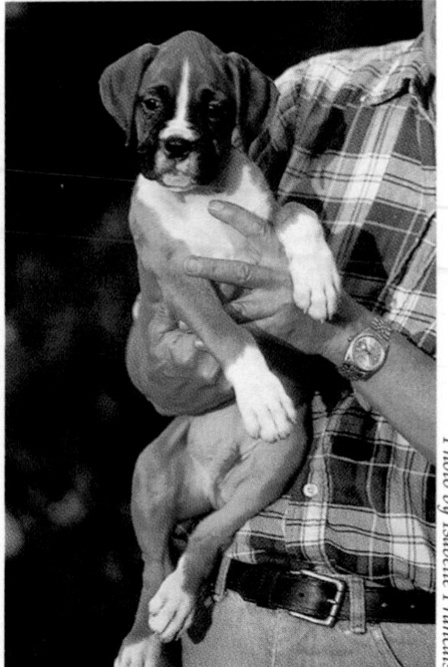

Photo by Isabelle Francais

As soon as your Boxer is old enough, take him with you wherever you go. Introducing him to new people, places, and experiences will ensure that your puppy is confident and well socialized.

THE EIGHTH WEEK

The eighth week of life is a frightening time for most puppies. Puppies go through several fear periods as they grow up, and this is the first one. Even though this is the traditional time during which most puppies go to their new homes, they would actually benefit by staying with their littermates for one more week. If the puppy leaves the breeder's home during this fear period and is frightened by the car ride home, he may retain that fear of car rides for the rest of his life. In fact, this very stress is why so many puppies do get carsick! This will also apply to the puppy's new home, his first trip to the veterinarian's office, or anything else that frightens him.

WEEKS NINE THROUGH TWELVE

The baby Boxer can go to his new home anytime during

Discipline is necessary at any age, but will be especially important during 9 to 12 weeks of age. You can show your Boxer his position in the family by laying him down and giving him a tummy rub; by baring his belly he is assuming a submissive position to you.

the ninth and tenth weeks of life. At this age, he is ready to form permanent relationships. Take advantage of this and spend time with your new puppy, playing with him and encouraging him to explore his new world. Teach him his name by calling him in a happier, higher-pitched tone of voice than normal. Encourage him to follow you by backing away from him, patting your leg, and using your voice.

Socialization is very important now, too. Socialization is more than simply introducing your puppy to other people, dogs, noises, and sounds. It is making sure your baby Boxer will not be frightened by these things as you introduce them. For example, once your baby Boxer has had some vaccinations (check with your veterinarian), take him with you to the pet store when you go to buy dog food. While there, introduce your puppy to the store clerks, other customers, and even to the store parrot. Your trip there could also include walking up some stairs, walking on slippery floors, and going through an automatic door. Things of this nature, introduced gradually and with encouragement and repeated all over town (on different days, of course) will add up to a confident, well-socialized puppy.

During this stage of development, your Boxer puppy's pack instincts are developing. He is beginning to understand which people belong to his pack (or family) and which don't. Do not let him growl at visitors during this stage; he is much too young to understand when and how to protect. Instead, stop the growling and let him know that you—as his pack leader—can protect the family.

You can show him his position in the family in several different ways, but one of the easiest is to lay him down, roll him over, and give him a tummy rub. This exercise may seem very simple, but by baring his tummy he is assuming a submissive position to you. When his mother corrected him by growling or barking at him, he would roll over and bare his tummy to her, in essence telling her, "Okay! I understand, you're the boss!" When you have him roll over for a tummy rub, you are helping him understand the same message, but are doing it in a very gentle, loving way.

Although your adolescent Boxer may try to assert his independence by breaking some rules, he must learn that you are the boss. Consistency in enforcing household rules is very important now.

Discipline is very important during this stage of development. Love, affection, and security are still important, too, of course, but right now your Boxer puppy needs to learn that his life is governed by some rules. Don't allow him to do anything now that you won't want him to continue doing later as a full-grown dog.

WEEKS THIRTEEN THROUGH SIXTEEN

From 13 through 16 weeks of age, your Boxer puppy will be trying to establish his position in your family pack. If you were able to set some rules in earlier stages of development, this won't be quite so difficult. However, if you caved in to that adorable puppy Boxer face, well, this could be a challenging time!

Consistency in enforcing household rules is very important now, and everyone in the family or household should be enforcing rules the same way. Boxers are very perceptive, and if your puppy

RETRIEVING

Begin retrieving games at nine to twelve weeks of age. Get your Boxer's attention with a toy he likes and then toss it four to six feet away. When he grabs the toy, call him back to you in a happy tone of voice. Praise him enthusiastically when he brings it back to you. If he runs away and tries to get you to chase him, stand up and walk away, stopping the game completely. Don't chase him. Let him learn now, while he's young, that he must play the game by your rules. Chasing a ball or soft flying disk can be great exercise for the puppy and can teach him to play by your rules, which sets the stage for a sound working relationship later.

Chasing a ball or retrieving a favorite toy is great exercise for a puppy and can also begin teaching him to follow your instructions, which sets the stage for a solid working relationship.

Photo by Isabelle Francais

senses a weak link in the chain of command, he will take advantage of it. This doesn't mean he's a bad puppy—it simply means he's a smart puppy.

Puppies with dominant personalities may begin mounting behavior toward small children in the family or toward the puppy's toys. Obviously, this is undesirable behavior and should be stopped immediately; just don't let it happen.

Socialization with other people, friendly dogs, and other similar experiences should continue throughout this stage of development.

A puppy should not be forced into situations he finds frightening. Respect his feelings and allow him to acclimate by giving him time and reassurance.

WEEKS SEVENTEEN THROUGH TWENTY SIX

Sometime between 17 and 26 weeks of age, most puppies go through another fear period, much like the one they went through at 8 weeks of age. Things the puppy had once accepted as normal may suddenly become frightening. A friend's Boxer walked into the backyard and began barking fearfully at the picnic table that had been in the same spot since before the puppy joined the family. It was as if the puppy had never noticed it before and all at once found it very scary.

Make sure you don't reinforce any of these fears. If you pet or cuddle him and tell him softly, "It's okay, don't be afraid," he will hear the soft words, feel the petting, and assume that these are positive reinforcements for his fears. In other words, your puppy will think he was right to be afraid. Instead, walk over to whatever is scaring him and touch it—letting him see you touch it—as you tell him, "Look at this!" in a happy tone of voice. Use a fun, playful tone of voice so that he can see that the thing he is afraid of really isn't scary at all.

Photo by Isabelle Francais

Although territorial instincts will continue to emerge as your Boxer develops, discourage aggressive behavior until your puppy matures. Too much emphasis at this stage could overemphasize overprotectiveness or fearfulness in your dog.

Your Boxer's protective instincts will continue to develop during this stage. If your Boxer continues to show protectiveness or aggression by growling, snarling, barking, or raising his hackles, interrupt his behavior by turning him away or distracting him. If you encourage this behavior too early, or if you correct it too harshly, you will overemphasize it, and your puppy may continue to do it. Too much emphasis at this stage may result in overprotectiveness or fearfulness in your dog as he grows up. Instead, react calmly and simply stop it from happening.

Boxers are naturally protective as adults, and if you wanted a Boxer because of this trait, don't worry about interrupting the behavior now. Training will not hamper those instincts. At this age, your Boxer puppy doesn't know what or when to protect. Instead of letting him take over (and learn bad habits), stop his behavior and let him know you are in charge. Later, when he's more mature, you can encourage the specific protectiveness you want.

THE TEENAGE MONTHS

The teenage months in a dog's life are very much like the teenage years in human children. Human adolescents are feeling strong and striving to prove their ability to take care of themselves. They want to be independent yet still want the security of home. These two conflicting needs seem to drive some teens (and their parents) absolutely crazy!

Dogs can be very much the same way. Boxers in adolescence push the boundaries of their rules, trying to see if you really will enforce them. Most Boxer owners say that during this stage of growing up their dogs act "too full of themselves."

With Boxers, the teenage stage usually hits at about 12 months of age, although it's not unusual to see it begin a month or two earlier. You'll know when it happens. One day you will ask your previously well-trained dog to do something he knows very

A puppy can get into a lot of mischief during his rebellious teenage months. Proper supervision and early obedience training can help stop problems before they start.

Photo by Isabelle Francais

well, like sit, and he'll look at you as if you're nuts. He's never heard that word before in his life and, even if he had, he still wouldn't do it!

Other common behaviors include regression in social skills. Your previously well-socialized Boxer may start barking at other dogs or jumping on people. He may start getting rough with children or may start chasing the cat.

During this stage of development, you really need to consistently enforce social and household rules. Hopefully, you will have already started obedience training, because that control will help. If you haven't started obedience training, do so now—don't wait any longer.

Make sure, too, that your dog regards you as the leader. This is not the time to try to be best friends—doing so would cause a dominant personality to regard you as weak. Instead, act like the leader. Stand tall when you relate to your dog. Bend over him (not down to him) when you pet him. You should always go first—through doorways or up the stairs—make him wait and then follow you. You should always eat before you feed your dog.

As the leader, you can give him permission to do things. For

As your Boxer puppy grows up, he will need care, kindness, and encouragement to become a well-adjusted adult.

example, if he picks up a toy and brings it to you to throw to him, give him permission to do it, "Good boy to bring me your toy!" If he lies down at your feet (by his own choice) tell him, "Good boy to lie down!" By giving him permission and praising him, you are putting yourself in control, even though he was already doing it of his own accord.

You need to understand that this rebellion is not directed at you, personally. Instead, it is a very natural part of growing up. Keep in mind that this, too, shall pass. Your Boxer will grow up—someday. Adolescence usually only lasts a few months (in dogs, anyway).

Photo by Isabelle Francais

Boxers are not usually considered fully mature—physically or mentally—until they are three years old.

GROWING UP

Boxers are not usually considered fully mature—mentally or physically—until they are three years old. And even then, some Boxers still behave like puppies for much longer. Usually, the bitches (females) act mature a little earlier than the males.

After the teenage stage but before maturity, your Boxer may go through another fear period. This generally hits at about 14 months of age, but may be later. Handle this one just like you did the others; don't reinforce your dog's fears. Happily, this is usually the last one your dog will have.

There may be another period of challenging—seeing if you really are the boss—at about two years of age. Treat this as you did the teenage stage; enforce the rules and praise what he does right.

When your Boxer reaches his third birthday, throw a party! He is considered grown up now. However, grown up to a Boxer doesn't always mean that life is serious. It will be when situations demand it; but in the meantime, life for a Boxer is about fun.

Early PUPPY Training

CRATE TRAINING

By about five weeks of age, most puppies are starting to toddle away from their mother and littermates to relieve themselves. You can use this instinct to keep the bed clean, and with the help of a crate, you can housetrain your Boxer puppy.

A crate is a plastic or wire travel cage that you can use as your Boxer's bed. Many new Boxer owners shudder at the thought of putting their puppy in a cage, "I could never do that!" they say. "It would be like putting my children in jail!" A puppy is not a child, however, and he has different needs and instincts. Puppies like to curl up in small, dark places. That's why they like to sleep under the coffee table or under a chair.

Because your Boxer puppy does have an instinct to keep his bed clean, being confined in the crate will help him develop more bowel and bladder control. When he is confined for gradually extended periods of time, he will hold his wastes to avoid soiling his bed. It is your responsibility to make sure he isn't left for too long.

The crate will also be your Boxer puppy's place of refuge. If he's tired, hurt, or sick, allow him to go back to his crate to sleep or hide. If he's overstimulated or excited, put him back in his crate to calm down.

Because the crate physically confines the puppy, it can also

BLANK SLATE

A young puppy's mind is like a blank slate, or in this era's terms, a newly formatted computer disk. What you teach your Boxer in his early months will have bearing on the puppy's behavior for the rest of his life. Therefore, it's important to keep in mind a vision of what your dog will grow up to be. Although Boxers are medium-sized dogs and not giant breeds, many do get quite large. They are strong, powerful dogs, and you need to be aware of this. At ten weeks of age, your Boxer puppy will enjoy a cuddle on your lap, but will you still want him to do that when he's 75 pounds of muscle and hard elbows? Teach him as a puppy what you want him to do as an adult.

Photo by Isabelle Francais

Teach your Boxer as a puppy what you want him to do as an adult. What he learns in his early months will have bearing on his behavior for the rest of his life.

prevent some unwanted behaviors, such as destructive chewing or raiding the trash cans. When you cannot supervise the puppy or when you leave the house, put him in his crate, and it will prevent him from getting into trouble.

Crate training is the easiest and fastest way to housetrain your Boxer puppy.

Photo by Isabelle Francais

Introducing the Crate

Introduce your puppy to the crate by propping open the door and tossing a treat inside. As you do this, tell your puppy, "Go to bed!" and let him go inside to get the treat. Let him investigate the crate and come and go as he wishes. When he's comfortable with that, offer

Photo by Isabelle Francais

The ideal place for the crate is in your bedroom—having you nearby during the night will give your Boxer puppy a feeling of security, whereas exiling him to another room will make him feel afraid and lonely.

him his next meal in the crate. Once he's in, close the door behind him, but let him out when he's through eating. Offer several meals in the same fashion; this will show your puppy that the crate is a pretty neat place.

After your Boxer puppy is used to going in and out of the crate for treats and meals, start feeding him back in his normal location and continue offering him a treat for going into the crate. Tell him, "Go to bed" and then give him his treat.

Don't let your puppy out of the crate if he throws a temper tantrum. If he starts crying, screaming, throwing himself at the door, or scratching at the door, correct him verbally, "No, quiet!" or simply close the door to the room and walk away. If you let him out after a tantrum, you will simply teach him that temper tantrums work. Instead, let him out when you are ready to let him out and when he is quiet.

Crate Location

The ideal place for the crate is in your bedroom, within arm's reach of the bed. This will give your Boxer eight uninterrupted hours with you while you do nothing but sleep. In these busy times, that is quality time. Having you nearby will also give your Boxer puppy a feeling of security, whereas exiling him to the laundry room or backyard will isolate him. He will be more apt to cry, whine, chew destructively, or get into other trouble because he is lonely or afraid.

Having the crate close by at night will save you some wear and tear, too. If he needs to go outside during the night (and he may need to for a few weeks), you will hear him whine and you can let him out before he has an accident. If he's restless or bored, you can rap on the top of his crate and tell him to be quiet without getting out of bed.

HOUSETRAINING

One of the most common methods of housetraining a puppy is paper training. The puppy is taught to relieve himself on newspapers and then, at some point, is retrained to go outside. However, paper training teaches the puppy to relieve himself in the house. Is that really what you want your Boxer to know?

Teach your Boxer what you want him to know now. Take

THERE ARE NO ACCIDENTS

If the puppy relieves himself in the house, it is not his fault—it's yours. That means the puppy was not supervised well enough or he wasn't taken outside in time. To the puppy, the act of relieving himself is very natural, so the idea that certain areas are unacceptable is foreign to him. His instincts tell him to keep his bed clean, but that's all. You need to teach him the correct places to go to prevent accidents. That requires supervision on your part.

If you take your puppy to the same place to eliminate every time, he will know what is expected of him. Reinforce what he has learned by praising him when he relieves himself in the correct area.

Photo by Isabelle Francais

PUNISHMENT

Do not try to housetrain your puppy by punishing him when he relieves himself in the house. If you scold him or rub his nose in his mess, you are not teaching him where he needs to relieve himself; you are, instead, teaching him that you think going potty is wrong. Because he has to go, he will then become sneaky about it and you will find puddles and piles in strange places. Keep in mind that the act of relieving himself is very natural; he has to do this. Instead of concentrating on correction, emphasize praise for going in the right place.

him outside to the place where you want him to relieve himself and tell him, "Go potty." (Use any command you'll be comfortable with.) When he has done what it is he needed to do, praise him.

Don't just open the door and send your puppy outside. How will you know that he has relieved himself? Go out with him so that you can teach him the command, praise him when he does it, and be sure he is done so it's safe to let him back inside. If he doesn't relieve himself when you take him out, it is not a problem, just put him back in his crate for a little while and take him back out later. Do *not* let him run around the house—even supervised—if he has not relieved himself outside.

Successful housetraining is based on setting your Boxer puppy up for success rather than failure. Keep accidents to a minimum and praise him when he does relieve himself in the correct area.

Establish a Routine

Boxers, like many other dogs, are creatures of habit and thrive on a routine. Housetraining is much easier if there is a set routine for eating, eliminating, playing, walking, training, and sleeping. A workable schedule might look like this:

Boxers are creatures of habit and thrive on routine, so to make training easier, set a schedule for eating, eliminating, playing, walking, and sleeping.

Photo by Isabelle Francais

6:00 am—Dad wakes up and takes the puppy outside. After the puppy relieves himself, Dad praises him and brings him inside. Dad fixes the puppy's breakfast, offers him water, and then sends him out into the backyard while he takes his shower.

7:00 am—Mom goes outside to play with the puppy for a few minutes before getting ready for work. Just before she leaves, she brings the puppy inside, puts him in his crate, and gives him a treat.

11:00 am—A dog-loving neighbor who is retired comes over. He lets the puppy out of his crate and takes him outside. The neighbor is familiar with the puppy's training, so he praises the puppy when he relieves himself. He throws the ball for the puppy, pets him, and cuddles him. When the puppy is worn out, he puts him back in his crate and gives him a treat.

3:00 pm—Daughter comes home from school and takes the puppy outside. She throws the ball for the puppy, picks up after him, and then takes the puppy for a walk. When they get back, she brings the puppy to her bedroom while she does her homework.

6:00 pm—Mom takes the puppy outside to go potty, praises him, and then feeds him dinner.

8:00 pm—After daughter plays with the puppy, she brushes him and then takes him outside to go potty.

11:00 pm—Dad takes the puppy outside for one last trip before bed.

The schedule you set up will have to work with your normal routine and lifestyle. Just keep in mind that your Boxer puppy should not remain in his crate for longer than three to four hours at a time, except during the night. In addition, the puppy will need to relieve himself after waking up, after eating, after playtime, and every three to four hours in between.

PATIENCE, PATIENCE, AND MORE PATIENCE

Boxer puppies need time to develop bowel and bladder control. Establish a routine that seems to work well for you and for your puppy, and then stick to it. Give your puppy time to learn and to grow up. If you stick to the schedule, your puppy will progress. However, don't let success go to your head. A few weeks without a mistake doesn't mean your Boxer puppy is housetrained; it means your routine is working. Too much freedom too soon will result in problems.

Photo by Isabelle Francais

By limiting your puppy's freedom, you can prevent accidents from occurring. If you can't supervise your Boxer, put him in his crate or outside in a fenced area.

Limit the Puppy's Freedom

Many puppies do not want to take the time to go outside to relieve themselves because everything exciting happens in the house. After all, that's where all the family members are. If your Boxer puppy is like this, you will find him sneaking off somewhere—behind the sofa or to another room—to relieve himself. By limiting the puppy's freedom, you can prevent some of these accidents. Close bedroom doors and use baby gates across hallways to keep him close. If you can't keep an eye on him, put him in his crate or outside.

HOUSEHOLD RULES

As mentioned before, it's important to start teaching your Boxer puppy the household

TIMING AGAIN

Do you walk your dog when he has to go potty? Many dog owners live in condos and apartments, so the dog must be taken for a walk in order to relieve himself. These dogs often learn that the walk is over once they go potty; therefore, they hold it as long as possible so that the walk will continue. To avoid this trap, encourage your puppy to relieve himself right away, praise him, and then continue the walk or outing for a little while afterward.

rules you wish him to follow as soon as possible. Your eight- to ten-week-old puppy is not too young to learn, and by starting early, you can prevent him from learning bad habits.

When deciding what rules you want him to learn, look at your Boxer puppy, not as the baby he is now, but as the adult he will grow up to be. Are you going to want him up on the furniture when he's 75 pounds of muscle, long legs, hard elbows, and rough paws? Do you want him to jump up on people? Given their own way, all Boxers jump up, waving those front paws. Do you want him to do that to the neighbor's children or to your grandmother?

Some common rules you may want to institute include teaching your Boxer not to jump on people, to behave when guests come to the house, to stay out of the kitchen, to leave the trash cans alone, and chew only on his own toys.

Teaching your Boxer puppy these rules is not difficult. Be very clear with your corrections. When he does something wrong, correct him with a deep, firm tone of voice, "No jump!" When he does something right, use a higher pitched tone of voice, "Good boy to chew on your toy!" You must be very clear—either something is right or it is wrong.

Patience, praise, and affection are the best motivators for your Boxer.

Photo by Isabelle Francais

Photo by Isabelle Francais

By starting obedience training early, you can keep your Boxer from learning bad habits.

ACCEPTING THE LEASH

Learning to accept the leash can be difficult for some puppies. If your Boxer puppy learns to dislike the leash as a young puppy, he may continue to resent it for many years. However, if he learns the leash is a key to more exciting things, he will welcome it.

Soon after you bring your puppy home, put a soft buckle collar on his neck. Make sure it's loose enough to come over his head if he gets tangled up in something. Give him a day or two to get used to the collar. Then, when you are going to be close by and can supervise him, snap the leash onto the collar and let him drag it behind him. As he walks around, he will step on the leash, feel it tug on his neck, and in doing so, will get used to the feeling of it.

After two or three short sessions like this, you can teach your puppy to follow you on the leash. Have a few pieces of a soft treat your puppy enjoys (soft so it can be easily chewed). Hold the leash in one hand and the treats in another. Show him the treat and back away a few steps as you tell your puppy, "Let's go! Good boy!" When he follows you a few steps, praise him and give him the treat. Boxer puppies are usually eagerly motivated by food, and when he learns a treat is being offered, he should follow you without any problem.

Photo by Isabelle Francais

Your Boxer must learn to accept a collar and leash for his safety as well as the safety of others.

Repeat the exercise two or three times and stop for this training session. Reward your puppy by giving him a tummy rub or by throwing the ball a few times. After several sessions like this, make it more challenging by backing away slowly or quickly, or by making turns. If he gets confused or balks, make it simple until he's willingly following you again.

INTRODUCING THE CAR

Many puppies are afraid of the car because a ride in the car was the first strange thing to

If your Boxer likes to pull you along when he's on a leash, try a no-pull training halter, guaranteed by the manufacturer to stop any dog, any size, any weight from pulling. Photo courtesy of Four Paws.

happen to them when they were taken from their mother and littermates. The car also takes them to the veterinarian's office, another strange place where someone in a white coat pokes them, prods them, and gives them vaccinations. You don't want this fear of the car to grab hold, though; you want your puppy to understand that riding in the car is something fun to do.

Start by lifting your puppy into the car and handing him a treat. As soon as he has finished the treat, lift him down and walk away. Repeat this simple exercise several times a day for a few days. Then lift him into the car, give him a treat, let him eat it, and then let him explore the car for a few minutes. After he has sniffed around a little, give him another treat, let him eat it, then lift him out of the car and walk away. Continue this training for a week or two, depending upon how nervous your puppy is in the car.

When your puppy has learned to expect a treat in the car, put his crate in the car and strap it down securely. Put your puppy in his crate, give him a treat, and then start the car's engine. Back down the driveway and then drive back up to the house. Stop the engine, give your puppy a treat, and let him out of his crate and the car. The next time, drive down the street and back, then go around the block. Increase the distance

IF YOUR PUPPY BALKS

If your puppy balks, do not use the leash to drag him to you. This will cause him to dig his feet in and apply the brakes. Instead, kneel down, open your arms wide, and encourage him to come to you, "Hey, Sweetie, here! Good boy!" When he dashes into your lap, praise him and tell him what a wonderful puppy he is. Then try the exercise again.

and time of the drives very gradually. Keep in mind that you want your puppy to expect good things in the car, not scary things. Your Boxer puppy will have a lifetime of car rides ahead of him, and life will be much nicer if he enjoys the rides.

END ON A HIGH NOTE

Always end all training sessions on a high note. If your Boxer puppy is worried, scared, or confused, help him to do something right and then end the training session with praise. Never end the session at a negative point or it will affect his outlook toward training later.

SOCIAL HANDLING

Your Boxer puppy cannot care for himself; you must be able to brush and comb him, bathe him, check his feet for cuts and scrapes, and clean his ears. Your Boxer puppy doesn't understand why you need to do these things that are annoying to him and he may struggle when you try to care for him. This social handling exercise will help teach your puppy to accept your care.

Your Boxer will have a lifetime of car rides ahead of him, so you don't want any fear associated with them. Train your puppy to expect good experiences in the car and he'll soon enjoy accompanying you on all kinds of road trips.

Sit down on the floor with your puppy and have him lie down between your legs. He can lie on his back or on his side; let him get comfortable. Start by giving him a slow, easy tummy rub; the idea here is to relax him. If your movements are fast and vigorous, you'll make him want to play. So keep it slow and gentle. If he starts to struggle, tell him calmly, "Easy. Be still." Restrain him gently if you need to do so.

When your puppy is relaxed, start giving him a massage. Start at his neck and ears, gently rubbing all around the base of each ear and working down the neck to the shoulders. Continue over his entire body, gently massaging it while, at the same time, checking his body for cuts, scratches, lumps, bumps, bruises, fleas, ticks, or any other problems that need to be taken care of.

Once your puppy has learned to enjoy this handling (very quickly!) you can—during the massage—clean his ears, wash out his eyes, trim his toenails, or do anything else that needs doing.

RELAX!

You can use the social handling exercise to relax your puppy when he's overstimulated. If you let him in from the backyard and he's full of Boxer energy, don't chase him down or try to correct him. Instead, sit down on the floor and invite him to join you. (Use a treat to get him to come to you if you need some extra incentive.) Once he's come to you, lay him down and begin the massage. He will relax and calm down, and in the process, will be receiving the attention he needs from you.

Bonding with your pet is an important building block in training, so be sure to spend some quality time with your Boxer after every session.

4 The Basic OBEDIENCE Commands

THE TEACHING PROCESS

Although Boxers are a very intelligent breed, you cannot simply tell your Boxer to do something and expect him to understand your verbal language. Training is a process that begins with teaching your dog that certain words have meanings and that you would like him to follow your directions. Your Boxer, however, doesn't understand why you want him to do these things; after all, why should he sit? He doesn't know why sit is so important to you. Therefore, training is a process.

Photo by Isabelle Francais

Your Boxer will pay more attention and try harder if he is praised for his efforts and rewarded for good behavior.

Show Your Dog

First, you want to show your dog what it is you want him to do and that there is a word—a human spoken sound—associated with that action or position. For example, when teaching him to sit, you can help him into position as you tell him, "Sit." Follow the command with praise, even if you helped him into position, "Good boy to sit!"

You will follow a similar pattern when teaching your dog most new things. If you want him off of the sofa, you can tell him, "Off the furniture," as you take him by the collar and pull him off. When he's off the furniture, tell him, "Good boy to get off the furniture."

Praise

Praise him every time he does something right, even if you help him do it. Your Boxer will pay more attention and try harder if he is praised for his efforts. However, don't give him undeserved praise; Boxers are very intelligent dogs and will quickly figure it out. Instead, give enthusiastic praise when he makes an effort and does something right for you.

Correct

Do not correct your dog until he understands what it is you want him to do. After he understands and is willing to obey the command, you can then correct him verbally or with a quick snap and release of the collar when he chooses *not* to do what you ask. Use *only* as much correction as is needed to get his attention and *no more.* With corrections, less is usually better, as long as your dog is responding.

Timing

The timing of your praise, corrections, and interruptions is very important. Praise him *as* he is doing something right. Correct him *when* he makes the mistake. Interrupt him *as* he starts to stick his nose into the trash can. If your timing is slow, he may not understand what you are trying to teach him.

Be Fair

Boxers resent corrections that are too harsh or unfair. They will show this resentment by refusing to work, by planting themselves and refusing to move, or by fighting back. Some Boxers will even show signs of

The basic obedience commands can be used to stop undesirable behavior—like digging in the garden. Use only as much correction as is needed to get your puppy's attention and remember to correct only when he makes a mistake, not after.

Photo by Isabelle Francais

A very intelligent breed, Boxers are enthusiastic and easily trainable. In fact, if you don't train your Boxer, he'll train you!

depression if a harsh training method continues.

SIT AND RELEASE

The sit command is the foundation for everything else your Boxer will learn. When your Boxer learns to sit and sit still, he learns to control himself. He learns that there are consequences to his actions. Learning self-control and understanding that he has control over the consequences of his actions is a very big lesson.

The sit is also a good alternative action for problem behavior. Your Boxer cannot sit still and jump on you at the

USE INTERRUPTIONS

Interrupt incorrect behavior as you see it happen. If your dog is walking by the kitchen trash can and turns to sniff it, interrupt him by saying, "Leave it alone!" If you tell him to sit and he does sit but then starts to get up, interrupt him, "No! Sit." By interrupting him, you can stop incorrect behavior before or as it happens.

Interruptions and corrections alone will not teach your Boxer; they are used to stop—at that moment—undesirable behavior or actions. Your Boxer learns much more when you reward his good behavior. Stop the behavior you don't want, but lavishly praise the actions you want to continue.

Teach your Boxer to sit by holding a treat in your hand and moving it from his head toward his tail. As his head goes up to follow your hand, his hips will go down into a sit. You can also shape him into a sit by sliding one hand down his hips and tucking his back legs under.

same time. He can do one or the other; therefore, learning to sit still for praise can replace jumping up on people for attention. He can't knock his food bowl out of your hand if he's sitting still, patiently waiting for his dinner. You can fasten a leash to his collar more easily if he's sitting still. This is a practical, useful command.

There are two basic methods of teaching your Boxer to sit. Some dogs work better with one technique than the other, so try both and see which is better for your puppy. Hold your Boxer's leash in your left hand and have some treats in your right hand. Tell him, "Sit!" as you move your right hand (with the treats) from his nose, over his head, and toward his tail. He will lift his head to watch your hand. As his head goes up and back, his hips will go down. As your Boxer sits, praise him, "Good boy to sit!" and give him a treat. Pet him in the sitting position.

When you are ready for your puppy to get up, tap him on the shoulder as you tell him, "Release!" Each exercise needs a beginning and an end. The sit command is the beginning and the release command tells him he is done and can now move. If he doesn't get up on his own, use your hands on his collar to walk him forward.

SIT, PLEASE!

Once your Boxer understands the sit command and is responding well, start having him sit for things that he wants. Have him sit while you hook a leash to his collar before a walk. Have him sit before you give him a treat, serve him his meals, or throw his ball. Boxers are working dogs and having your Boxer sit can be his first job!

If your Boxer is too excited by the treats to think (and some Boxers are like that), put the treats away. Tell your Boxer to sit as you place one hand under his chin on the front of his neck, and you slide the other hand down his hips to tuck his back legs under. Gently shape him into a sit as you give him the command, "Sit." Praise him and release him.

If your dog is wiggly as you try to teach this exercise, keep

ONE COMMAND

Don't keep repeating any command. The command should not be, "Sit! Sit, sit, *sit*, please sit. *Sit*!" If you give repeated commands for the sit, your Boxer will assume that method will apply to everything else. Tell him once to sit and then help him do it if he doesn't obey.

Photos by Vince Serbin

When teaching the down exercise, start with your Boxer in the sit/stay position, then have him follow a treat to the ground as you give the command. Let him have the treat when he reaches the down position.

your hands on him. If he pops up, interrupt that action with a deep, firm tone of voice, "Be still!" When he responds and stops wiggling, praise him quietly and gently.

DOWN

The down exercise continues one of the lessons the sit command started, that of self-control. It is hard for many energetic, bouncy, young Boxers to control their own actions, but it is a lesson all dogs must learn. Practicing the down exercise teaches your Boxer to lie down and be still.

Start with your Boxer in a sit. Rest one hand gently on his shoulder and have a treat in the other hand. Let him smell the treat and then tell him, "Down" while you take the treat straight down to the ground in front of his paws. As he follows the treat down, place your hand on his shoulders to encourage him to lie down. Praise him, give him the treat, and then have him hold the position for a moment. Then release him in the same way you did from the sit—pat him on the shoulder, tell him "Release!" and let him get up. If your dog looks at the treat as you make the signal, but doesn't follow the treat to the ground, simply scoop his front legs up and forward as you lay him down. The rest of the exercise is the same.

As your Boxer learns what the down command means, you can have him hold it a few minutes longer before releasing him, but do not step away from him yet. Stay next to him and if he's wiggly, keep your hand on his shoulder to help him stay in position.

Once each day, have your Boxer lie down and then before you release him, roll him over for a tummy rub. He will enjoy the tummy rub, relax a little, and will learn to enjoy the down position. This is especially important for young Boxers that want to do anything *but* lie down and hold still.

BE FAIR

Make sure you are very clear as to what you want your dog to do. Remember, something is either right or wrong to your dog—it's not partially right or partially wrong. Be fair with your commands, your praise, and your corrections.

STAY

When your Boxer understands both the sit and down commands, you can introduce him to the stay exercise. You want to convey to your Boxer that the word

Aside from having very practical uses, the stay command teaches your Boxer self-control.

Photo by Isabelle Francais

Photo by Vince Serbin

Hand signals used in conjunction with verbal commands can be very effective when teaching your Boxer basic obedience.

"stay" means "hold still." When your dog is sitting and you tell him to stay, you want him to remain in the sitting position until you go back to him and release him. When you tell him to stay while he's lying down, you want him to remain lying down until you go back to him to release him from that position. Eventually, he will be able to hold the sit position for several minutes and the down position for even longer.

Start by having your Boxer sit. Holding the leash in your left hand, use it to put a slight bit of pressure backward (toward his tail) as you tell him, "Stay." At the same time, use your right hand to give your dog a hand signal that will mean stay—an open-hand gesture with the palm toward your dog's face. Take one step away and, at the same time, release the pressure on the leash. If your dog moves or gets up, tell him "No!" so that he knows he made a mistake and put him back into position. Repeat the exercise. After a few seconds, go back to him and praise him. Don't let him move from position until you give him the release command. Use the same process to teach the stay command in the down position.

With the stay command, you always want to go back to your Boxer to release him. Don't release him from a distance or call him to come to you from the stay position. If you do either of these, your dog will be much less reliable on the stay; he will continue to get up from the stay because you will have taught him to do exactly that. When teaching the stay, you want your Boxer to learn that "stay" means "Hold this position until I come back to you to release you." No confusion and no questions asked.

As your Boxer learns the stay command, you can *gradually* increase the time you ask him to hold the position. However,

Photo by Isabelle Francais

Your Boxer should be able to remain in position until you release him.

USING THE STAY COMMAND

You can use the stay command around the house. For example, in the evening when you're watching a favorite television show, have your Boxer lie down at your feet while you sit on the sofa. Give him a toy to chew on and tell him, "Stay." Have him do a down/stay when guests visit so he isn't jumping all over them. Have him lie down and stay while the family is eating so he isn't begging under the table. There are a lot of practical uses for the stay command; just look at your normal routine and see where it can work for you.

if your dog is making a lot of mistakes or moving often, you are either asking your dog to hold it too long, or your dog doesn't understand the command yet. In either case, go back and teach the exercise again from the beginning. Increase the distance you move away from your dog very gradually, as well. Again, if your dog is making a lot of mistakes, you're moving away too quickly. Teach everything one step at a time.

When your Boxer understands the stay command but chooses not to do it, you need to let him know that the

Eye contact is an essential element in training. The watch me exercise teaches your Boxer to ignore distractions and focus on you.

command is not optional. Many young, wiggly Boxers want to do anything but hold still; however, holding still is very important to Boxer owners. Correct excess movement with your voice, "No! Be still! Stay!" and if that doesn't work, use a verbal correction and a snap and release of the leash. When he does control himself, praise him enthusiastically.

WATCH ME

The watch me exercise teaches your Boxer to ignore distractions and pay attention to you. This is particularly useful when you're out in public and your dog is distracted by children playing or dogs barking behind a fence.

Start the exercise by having your Boxer sit in front of you. Have a treat in your right hand. Let him sniff it and then tell him, "Sweetie, watch me!" as you take the treat from his nose up to your chin. When his eyes follow the treat in your hand and he looks at your face, praise him, "Good boy to watch me!" and give him the treat. Then release him from the sit. Repeat the exercise again exactly the same way two or three times and quit for that training session.

Because this is hard for young, bouncing Boxers, practice initially at home where there are few distractions. Once he knows the exercise well indoors, you need to try it outside where there are

Keep training sessions short and always remember to praise your Boxer when he obeys a command, even if you had to help him do it.

many more things to distract him. Take him out in the front yard (on leash, of course) and tell him to watch you. If he ignores you, take his chin in your left hand (treat is in the right) and hold it so that he must look at your face. Praise him, even though you are helping him do it.

Once your dog will watch you outside despite some distractions, move on to the next training step. Have him sit in front of you and tell him to watch you. As he watches you, take a few steps backward and ask him to follow you while you're walking. Praise him when he does. Try it again. When he can follow you six or seven steps and watch you at the same time, make it more challenging—back up, turn to the left or right, or zigzag. Praise him when he continues to watch you.

HEEL

You want your Boxer to learn that heel means "Walk by my left side, with your neck and shoulders by my left leg, and maintain that position." Ideally, your Boxer should maintain that position as you walk slowly, quickly, turn corners, or weave in and out through a crowd.

To start, practice a watch me exercise to get your dog's attention focused on you. Back away from him and encourage him to follow you. When he does, simply turn your body—as you are backing up—so that your dog ends up on your left side and continue walking. If you have done this correctly, it will be one smooth movement so you and your dog end up walking forward together with your dog on your left side.

The heel exercise teaches your dog to walk beside you without pulling, which will make your daily outings together more enjoyable.

Let's walk it through in slow motion. Sit your dog in front of you and do a watch me. Back away from your dog and encourage him to follow you. As he's watching you, turn toward your left as you are

Photo by Vince Serbin

The come command is one of the most important commands your Boxer needs to learn; it could also be a lifesaver someday.

backing up; continue turning in that direction so you and your dog end up walking forward together. Your dog should end up on your left side (or you should end up on your dog's right side).

If your dog starts to pull forward, simply back away from him and encourage him to follow you. If you need to do so, use the leash with a snap and release motion to make the dog follow you. Praise him when he does. Don't hesitate to go back and forth—walking forward and then backing away several times—if you need to do so. In fact, sometimes this can be the best exercise you can do to get your dog's attention focused on you.

When your dog is walking with you nicely and paying attention to you, you can start to eliminate the backing away. Start the heel command with your Boxer sitting by your left side. Tell him, "Sweetie, watch me! Heel." Start walking. When he walks nicely with you, praise him. However, if he gets distracted or starts to pull, simply back away from him again.

COME

The come command is one of the most important commands your Boxer needs to learn. Not only is the come command important around the house in your daily routine, but it could also be a lifesaver someday, especially if he decides to dash into the street when a car is coming. Because this command is so important, you will use two different techniques to teach your dog to come to you when you call him.

Photo by Isabelle Francais

In the early stages of training, treats are a great way to motivate your Boxer to learn. Once he knows the basic commands, you can wean him from the treats.

With a Treat

The first technique will use a sound stimulus and a treat to teach your Boxer to come to you when you call him. Take a small plastic container (such as a margarine container) and put a handful of dry dog food in it. Put the lid on and shake it. It should make a nice rattling sound.

Do you remember those silent dog whistles that used to be advertised in comic books? There was nothing magical about those whistles except that they were so high pitched that dogs could hear them but people couldn't. The container we're using to teach the come command works on the same principle that the silent dog whistle does—it's a sound stimulus you can use to get the dog's attention so that you can teach him. By teaching him to pay attention to the sound of the shaker and by teaching him that the sound of the shaker means he's going to get a treat, we can make the come command that much more exciting. Your dog will be more likely to come to you (especially when there are distractions) if he's excited about it.

Have the shaker in one hand and some good dog treats in the other. Shake the container and as your Boxer looks at it and at you, ask him, "Cookie?" Use whatever word he already knows for a treat. I use the word cookie, but you can use anything he already

DON'T USE THE COME COMMAND AS PUNISHMENT

Never call your dog to come and then punish him for something he did earlier. Not only is the late punishment ineffective (it always is), but that unfair punishment will teach your dog to avoid you when you call him. Keep the come command positive all the time!

understands. When you say "cookie," pop a treat in his mouth. Do it again. Shake, shake, "Cookie?" and pop a treat in his mouth. The sound of the container, your verbal question, and the treat are all becoming associated with the command in your dog's mind. He is learning that the sound of the container equals the treat—an important lesson! Do this several times a day for several days.

After a few days of practice, with your dog sitting in front of you, replace the word "cookie" with the word "come." Shake the container, say "Come," and pop a treat in his mouth. You are rewarding him even though he didn't actually come to you—he was still sitting in front of you. However, you are teaching him that the sound of the shaker now equals the word "come" and he still gets the treat. Another important

When teaching the come command, you can use a long line or a retractable leash. It will provide the dog with freedom while allowing the owner complete control. Leashes are available in a wide variety of lengths for all breeds of dog. Photo courtesy of Flexi-USA, Inc.

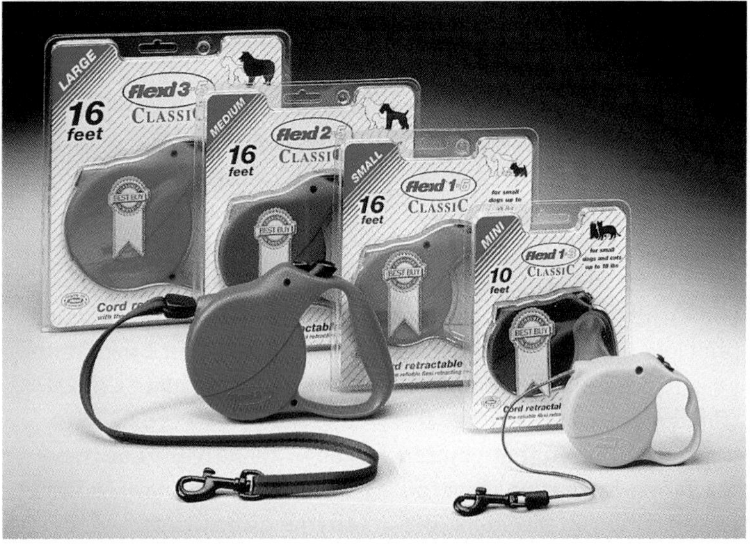

lesson. Do this several times a day for several days.

When your Boxer is happy to hear the shaker and is drooling to get a treat, start calling him from across the room. Shake the container as you say, "Come!" When he dashes to you, continue to give him a treat as you praise him, "Good boy to come!" Practice this up and down the hallway, inside and outside, and across the backyard. Make it fun; keep up with the treats and the verbal praise.

Never allow your Boxer off-leash freedom until he reliably and consistently obeys your commands.

The Come With a Long Line

The second method of teaching your dog to come uses a long leash or a length of clothesline rope. Because Boxers are athletic and fast, have a line at least 30 feet in length. Fasten the line to your Boxer's collar and then let him go play. When he is distracted by something, call him to come, "Sweetie, come!" If he responds and comes right away, praise him. If he doesn't respond right away, do *not* call him again. Pick up the line, back away from him, and using the line, make him come to you. Do not give him a verbal correction at this time; he may associate the verbal correction with coming to you. Instead, simply make him come to you even if you have to drag him in with the line.

DON'T WORRY

Some people have reservations about using food treats because they are worried the dog will not come to them when they don't have a treat. First of all, you will use two different techniques to teach the come command and only one technique uses the treats. Second, even with this technique, you will eventually stop using treats. Also, using this method when first introducing the come command produces such a strong, reliable come response, that it's worth all of your efforts.

Let him go again, and repeat the entire exercise. Make sure you always praise him when he does decide to come to you. If he is really distracted, use the shaker and treats along with the long line, especially in the early stages of training. You can always wean him from the treats later; right now let's make the come command work.

Don't allow your Boxer to have freedom off the leash until he is grown up enough to handle the responsibility and is very well trained. Many dog owners let their dogs off leash much too soon and the dogs learn bad habits that their owners wish they hadn't. Each time your dog learns that he can ignore you or run away from you, it reinforces the fact that he can. Instead, let him run around and play while dragging the long line. That way you can always regain control when you need to.

USE IT OR LOSE IT!

The best way to make this training work for you and your Boxer is to use it. Training is not just for those training sessions; instead, training is for daily life. Incorporate it into your everyday routine. Have your Boxer sit before you feed him. Have him lie down and stay while you eat. Have him sit and stay at the gate while you take the trash cans out. Have him do a down/stay when guests come over. Use these commands as part of your daily life. They will work much better that way.

Training your Boxer is a learning process that requires time, dedication, and determination.

5 All About FORMAL Training

Many dog owners won't admit that their dog needs training. "He does everything I ask," they say. Yet, when asked specific questions about behavior, the answer changes. A trained Boxer won't jump up on people, dash out the open door, or raid the trash can.

Dog owners can benefit from training, too. During training, they learn how to teach their dogs and how to motivate them to behave so that good behavior can be encouraged. They also learn how to prevent problem behavior from happening and how to correct the mistakes that do occur.

Training helps to strengthen the loving relationship between dog and owner.

WHY IS TRAINING IMPORTANT?

When you decided to add a Boxer to your family, you probably did so because you wanted a companion, a friend, a protector, and a confidant. You may have wanted a dog to go for walks with you, to run along the beach, to catch tennis balls, and to hike in the mountains. You may have wanted your children to have the same relationship with a dog that you remember from your childhood. To do any of these things, your Boxer will need training.

Dog training is much more than the traditional sit, down, stay, and come. Dog training means teaching your Boxer that he's living in your house, not his. It means that you can set some rules and expect him to follow them. It will not turn your Boxer into a robot; but instead, it will teach your Boxer to look at you in a new light. Training will cause you to look at him differently, too. Dog training is not

Photo by Isabelle Francais

When looking for a training class, talk to instructors about their training methods and experience. Also, ask other pet owners for recommendations.

something you do *to* your Boxer—it's something you do together.

TRAINING METHODS

Talk to a dozen dog trainers (someone who trains dogs) or dog obedience instructors (someone who teaches the dog owner how to teach his dog), ask them how they train, and you will get a dozen different answers. Any trainer or instructor who has been in the business for any period of time is going to devise a method or technique that works best for her. Each method will be based on the trainer's personality, teaching techniques, experience, and philosophy regarding dogs and dog training. Any given method may work wonderfully for one trainer, but may fail terribly for another.

Because there are so many different techniques, styles, and methods, choosing a particular instructor may be difficult. It is important to understand some of the different training methods so that you can make a reasonable decision.

Compulsive Training

Compulsive training is regarded as a method of training that forces the dog to behave. This is usually a correction-based training style, sometimes with forceful corrections. This training is often used with law enforcement and military dogs and can be quite effective with hard-driving, strong-willed dogs. Many pet owners do not like this style of training and tend to feel it is too rough.

Inducive Training

This training is exactly the opposite of compulsive training. Instead of being forced to do something, the dog is induced or motivated toward proper behavior. Depending upon the instructor, there are few or no corrections used. This training works very well for most puppies, for softer dogs, and sometimes for owners who dislike corrections of any kind.

Unfortunately, this is not always the right technique for all Boxers. Many Boxers will take advantage of the lack of corrections or discipline. Some very intelligent dogs with dominant personalities (including some Boxers) look upon the lack of discipline as weakness on your part and will set their own rules, which may not be the rules you wish to enforce.

Somewhere in the Middle

The majority of trainers and instructors use a training method that is somewhere in between both of these techniques. An inducive method is used when possible, while corrections are used only as needed. Obviously, the range can be vast, with some trainers leaning toward more corrections and others using as few corrections as possible.

GROUP CLASSES OR PRIVATE LESSONS

There are benefits and drawbacks to both group classes and private lessons. In group classes, the dog must learn to behave around other distractions, specifically, the other dogs and people in class.

A group training class is a great way to learn basic obedience and a perfect place for your Boxer to improve his social skills.

Because the world is made up of lots of things capable of distracting your Boxer, this can work very well. In addition, a group class can work like group therapy for dog owners. The owners can share triumphs and mishaps and can encourage and support one another. Many friendships have begun in group training classes.

The drawback to group classes is that the distractions of a group class are too much. Some dogs simply cannot concentrate at all, especially in the beginning of training. For these dogs, a few private lessons may help enough that the dog can join a group class later on. Dogs with severe behavior problems—especially aggression—should bypass group classes for obvious reasons.

Private lessons—one-on-one training with the owner, dog, and instructor—are also good for people with a very busy schedule who may otherwise not be able to do any training at all.

GOALS FOR YOUR BOXER

What do you want training to accomplish? Do you want your Boxer to be calm and well-behaved around family members? Do you want him to behave himself in public? Would you like to participate in dog activities and sports? There are an unlimited number of things you can train your Boxer to do; it's up to you to decide what you would like to do and to find a training program to help you achieve those goals. Then, as you start training, talk to your trainer about them so she can guide you in the right direction.

PUPPY CLASS

Puppy or kindergarten classes are for puppies over 10 weeks of age, but not over 16 weeks. These classes are half obedience training and half socialization. For young puppies, both of these subjects are very important. The puppy's owner learns how to prevent problem behaviors from occurring and how to establish household rules.

BASIC OBEDIENCE CLASS

This class is for puppies that have graduated from a puppy class, for puppies over four months of age that haven't attended a puppy class, or for adult dogs. In this class, the dogs and their owners work on basic obedience commands, including sit, down, stay,

Photo by Isabelle Francais

First-time dog owners should consider signing up for puppy classes. An experienced trainer can teach you how to prevent problem behaviors from occurring and how to establish household rules.

come, and heel. Most instructors also spend time discussing problem prevention and problem solving, especially common problems like jumping on people, barking, digging, and chewing.

ADVANCED TRAINING

Advanced training classes will vary depending upon the instructor. Some offer classes designed to teach you how to control your dog off leash, some emphasize dog sports, and others may simply continue basic training skills. Ask the instructor what she offers.

DOG SPORTS TRAINING

Some instructors offer training for one or more of the various dog activities or sports. There are classes to prepare you for competition in obedience trials, conformation dog shows, flyball, agility, or schutzhund. Other trainers may offer training for noncompetitive activities, such as therapy dog work.

FINDING AN INSTRUCTOR OR TRAINER

When trying to find an instructor or trainer, word-of-mouth referrals are probably

Once your Boxer masters basic obedience, he can go on to compete in more advanced activities, like agility or conformation trials.

Photo by Karen Taylor

Both you and your Boxer should feel comfortable with the instructor and his training methods.

the best place to start. Although instructors can place an advertisement in the newspaper or yellow pages, the ad itself is no guarantee of quality or expertise. However, happy customers will demonstrate their experience with well-behaved dogs and will be glad to tell you where they received instruction.

Have you admired a neighbor's well-behaved dog? Ask where they went for training. Call your veterinarian, local pet store, or groomer and ask who they recommend. Make notes about each referral. What did people like about this trainer? What did they dislike?

Once you have a list of referrals, start calling instructors and ask them a few questions. How long has she been teaching dog obedience classes? You will want a trainer with experience, of course, so that she can handle the various situations that may arise. However, experience alone is not the only qualification. Some people that have been training for years are still teaching exactly the same way they did many years ago and have never learned anything new.

Ask the instructor about Boxers. What does she think of the breed? Ideally, she should be knowledgeable about the breed, what makes them tick,

BUILDING A RELATIONSHIP

Training builds a relationship between you and your dog. This relationship is built on mutual trust, affection, and respect. Training can help your dog become your best friend, a well-behaved companion who is a joy to spend time with and one who won't send your blood pressure sky-high!

and how to train them. If she doesn't like the breed, go elsewhere.

Ask the instructor to explain her training methods. Does this sound like something you would be comfortable with? Ask if any alternative methods are used. Not every dog will respond the same way, so every instructor should have a backup plan.

Does the instructor belong to any professional organizations? The National Association of Dog Obedience Instructors (NADOI) and the Association of Pet Dog Trainers (APDT) are two of the more prominent groups. Both of these organizations publish regular newsletters to share information, techniques, new developments, and more. Instructors that belong to professional organizations are more likely to be up-to-date on training techniques, styles, and so forth, as well as information about specific dog breeds.

Make sure, too, that the instructor will be able to help you achieve your goals. For example, if you want to compete in obedience trials, she should have experience in that field and knowledge of the rules and regulations concerning that competition.

After talking to the trainer or instructor, ask if you can watch her training class. If she says no, then cross her off your list. There should be no reason why you cannot attend one class to see if you will be comfortable with this instructor and her style of teaching. As you watch the class, see how she handles the students' dogs. Would you let her handle your dog? How does she relate to the students? Are they relaxed? Do they look like they're having a good time? Are they paying attention to her?

After watching a class and talking to the instructor, you should be able to make a decision as to which class you want to attend. If you're still undecided, call the instructor back and ask a few more questions. After all, you are hiring her to provide a service and you must be comfortable with your decision.

6 Advanced TRAINING and Dog Sports

You are never finished with dog training, especially if you and your Boxer enjoy the time spent together. There is always more to learn. You can teach your dog hand signals, to listen to you off leash, or even some tricks. There is a lot you can do together, including a number of different dog activities and sports. Before you begin any of these exercises or activities, however, make sure your Boxer is proficient in all of the basic commands. If he's having trouble with some of these commands, go back, review them, and practice them.

HAND SIGNALS

When you start teaching hand signals, keep a treat in your hand to get your Boxer's attention and use the verbal command he already knows to help him understand what you are trying to tell him. As he responds, decrease the verbal command to a whisper and emphasize the hand signal.

The difficult part of teaching hand signals is that, in the

Boxers are athletic and well-balanced dogs that require physical activity. Participating in dog sports or competition is something you can enjoy together.

Photo by Isabelle Francais

Before beginning advanced training, your Boxer must be proficient in the basic commands. If he is having trouble with any of these commands, go back, review, and practice them.

beginning, your dog may not understand that these movements of your hand and arm have any significance. After all, people "talk" with their hands all the time; hands are always moving and waving. Dogs learn early to ignore hand and arm movements. Therefore, to make hand signals work, your Boxer needs to watch you. Having a good treat in the hand that is making the movement can help.

Down

When you taught your Boxer to lie down using the treat by taking it from his nose to the ground in front of his front paws, you were teaching him a hand signal. Granted, he was watching the treat in your hand, but he was also getting used to seeing your hand move. Therefore, switching him over from a verbal command to a hand-signal-only command should be easy.

Have your dog sit in front of you. Verbally, tell him "Down" as you give him the hand signal to go down (with a treat in your hand), just as you did when you were originally teaching it. When he lies down, praise him and then release him. Practice it a

To make hand signals work, your Boxer must watch you and understand that these specific movements of your arm and hand have significance.

Photo by Vince Serbin

Hand signals will help your Boxer follow commands from a distance and can be useful in many different situations, both at home and in unfamiliar environments.

few times. Now, give him the signal to go down (with a treat in your hand), but do not give a verbal command. If he lies down, praise him, give him the treat, and release him. If he does not go down, give the leash a slight snap and release down toward the ground—not hard, but just enough to let him know, "Hey! Pay attention!" When he goes down, praise and release him.

When your dog can reliably follow the hand signal without a verbal command, make it more challenging. Signal him to lie down when you are across the room from him. Signal him to lie down while you're talking to

USING HAND SIGNALS

Dog owners often think of hand signals as something that only a very advanced dog can respond to and that is partially right. It does take some training. However, hand signals are useful for all dog owners. For example, if your dog responds to hand signals, you can give him the signal to go lie down while you're talking on the telephone and you won't have to interrupt your conversation to do so.

someone. Signal him to lie down when there are some distractions around him. Remember to praise him enthusiastically when he goes down on the signal.

Sit

If you were able to teach your Boxer to sit using a treat above his nose, you were teaching him to sit using a hand signal. If you had to teach him by shaping him into a sit, don't worry—we can still teach him a signal.

With your Boxer on leash, hold the leash in your left hand and a treat in your right hand. Stand in front of your Boxer and take the treat from his nose upward. At the same time, whisper "Sit." When he sits, praise him and release him. Try it again. When he is watching your hand and sitting reliably, stop whispering the command and let him follow the signal. If he doesn't sit, jiggle the leash and collar to remind him that something is expected. Again, when he sits, praise him.

Stay

When you taught the stay command you used a hand signal, the open-palm gesture toward your Boxer's face. This signal is so obvious your dog will probably do it without any additional training. Have your dog sit or lie down and tell him "stay" using only the hand signal. Did he hold it? If he did, go back to him and praise him. If he didn't, use the leash to correct him (snap and release) and try it again.

Come

You want the hand signal for the come command to be a very broad, easily seen signal—one that your dog can recognize even if he's distracted by something. Therefore, this signal will be a wide swing of the right arm, starting with your arm held straight out to your side from the shoulder and horizontal to the ground. The motion will be to bring the hand to your chest following a wide wave—as if you were reaching out to get your dog and bring him to you.

Start teaching the signal by having a shaker in your right hand as you start the signal. Shake it slightly to get your dog's attention and then complete the signal. Praise your dog when he responds and comes to you. If he doesn't respond right away, start the signal again and this time tell him (verbally) to come as you make the signal (and shake the shaker). Again, praise him when he comes. Gradually eliminate the verbal command, and when your Boxer is responding well, gradually stop using the shaker.

OFF-LEASH CONTROL

One of the biggest mistakes many dog owners make is to take their dogs off the leash too soon. When you take your dog off the leash, you have very little control and only your previous training can help control his behavior. Also, if you take your dog off leash before you have established enough control or before your dog is mentally mature enough to accept that control, you are setting yourself up for disaster.

Boxers are smart, curious dogs and they love to check out new things, especially new smells. A rabbit, butterfly, or bird was made to chase, as far as Boxers are concerned. More than one Boxer has been so involved in his exploring that he's forgotten to pay attention to his owner's commands. Before your Boxer is allowed to be off leash (outside of a fenced yard or your backyard), you need to make sure your dog's training is sound, which means he should be responding reliably and well to all of the basic commands.

Your Boxer must also be mentally mature, and in some Boxers that might be two, two and a half, or even three years of age. He should be past the challenging teenage stage of development. Never take an adolescent off leash outside of a fenced-in area; that is setting the young dog up for problems.

If your Boxer doesn't respond when you call him, don't repeat the command or beg him to come. Instead, use a long line to make him do it. Your Boxer needs to learn that come is not an optional command.

The Come Command on a Long Line

The long line (or leash) that was introduced earlier in the section on teaching the come command is also a good training technique to prepare your dog for off-leash control. Review that section and practice the come command on the long line until you are comfortable that your dog understands the command from 20 to 30 feet

Although you shouldn't let your Boxer off leash in public places, teaching your dog to heel without a leash is a good way to avert possible hazards.

away (the length of the long line) and will do it reliably.

Now take your Boxer out to play in a different place that is safe and free from danger—a school yard is good. Let him drag the line behind him as he sniffs and explores. When he's distracted and not paying attention to you, call him to come. If he responds right away, praise him enthusiastically. Tell him what a smart, wonderful dog he is. If he doesn't respond right away, step on the end of the long line, pick it up, and back away from your dog, calling him again as you use the long line to make him come to you. Don't beg him to come to you; don't repeat the come command over and over. Simply use the line to make him do it. The come is not an optional command!

Heel

In most public places, dogs are required to be on a leash; however, teaching your Boxer to heel without a leash is a good exercise. Not only is it a part of obedience competition (for people interested in that sport), but it's a good practical command, too. What would happen if your dog's leash or collar broke when you were out for a walk? Accidents happen and if your dog has already been trained to heel off leash, disaster will be averted.

To train for this, hook two leashes up to your dog's collar. Use your regular leash and a lightweight leash. Do the watch me command with treats and then tell your dog to heel. Practice a variety of things: walk slow, walk fast, turn corners, and perform figure eights. When your dog is paying attention well, reach down and unhook his regular leash, tossing it to the ground in front of him. If he bounces up, assuming he's free, correct him with the second leash, "Hey! I didn't release you!" and make him sit in the heel position. Hook his regular leash back up and repeat the exercise. When he doesn't take advantage of the regular leash being removed, then tell him to heel and continue practicing the exercise. Do not use the second leash for minor correction, save it for control. If he tries to dash away, pull from you, or otherwise break the heel position, use that second leash for control and hook his regular leash back on again.

Repeat this, going back and forth between one leash and two, until he's not even thinking about whether his regular leash is on or not. You want him to work reliably without questioning the leash's control. For some Boxers, this may take several weeks worth of work. When he is working reliably, put the second leash away. Take his regular leash, hook it up to his collar, and fold it up. Tuck it under his collar between his shoulder blades so that it is lying on his back. Practice his

The Boxer is capable of being an impressive presence in the show ring. When competing in conformation events, he will be judged on how closely he conforms to the standard for the breed.

Photo by Isabelle Francais

heel work. If he makes a mistake, grab the leash and collar as a handle and correct him. When the correction is over, take your hand off.

Expect and demand the same level of obedience off leash that you do on leash. Don't make excuses for off-leash work.

DOG SPORTS

Do you like training your Boxer? If you and your Boxer are having a good time, you may want to try one or more dog activities or sports. There are a lot of different things you can do with your dog—some are competitive, some are fun, some do good works—what you decide to do depends upon you and your dog.

Conformation Competition

The American Kennel Club (AKC) and the United Kennel Club (UKC) both award conformation championships to purebred dogs. The requirements vary between the registries, but basically a championship is awarded when a purebred dog competes against other dogs of his breed and wins. When competing, the judge compares each dog against a written standard for his breed and chooses the dog that most closely represents that standard of excellence.

This is a very simplistic explanation; however, if you feel your Boxer is very handsome, you may want to go watch a few local dog shows. Observe the Boxers competing and talk to some of the Boxer owners and handlers. Does your Boxer still look like a good candidate? You will also want to do some reading about your breed, about conformation competition, and perhaps even attend a conformation class.

Obedience Competition

Obedience competition is a team sport involving you and

Obedience competition is a team sport in which both you and your Boxer are judged on how well you complete a specific set of exercises.

Photo by Isabelle Francais

your Boxer. There are set exercises that must be performed in a certain way, and both you and your dog are judged as to your abilities to perform these exercises. Both the AKC and the UKC sponsor obedience competitions for all breeds of dog, as do some other organizations, including the Boxer Club of America. There are also independent obedience competitions or tournaments held all over the country.

Before you begin training to compete, write to the sponsoring organization and get a copy of the rules and regulations pertaining to competitions. Go to a few local dog shows and watch the obedience competitions. See who wins and who doesn't. What did they each do differently? There are also a number of books on the market that specifically address obedience competition. You may want to find a trainer in your area who specializes in competition training.

Canine Good Citizen

The Canine Good Citizen (CGC) program was instituted by the AKC in an effort to promote and reward responsible dog ownership. During a CGC test, the dog and owner must complete a series of ten exercises, including sitting for petting

A good canine citizen must learn to get along with other animals and people. This Boxer has certainly passed the test with flying colors.

Photo by Isabelle Francais

AGILITY

Agility is a fast-paced sport. Dogs must complete a series of obstacles correctly in a certain period of time, and the dog with the fastest time wins. Obstacles might include tunnels, hurdles, an elevated dog walk, and more. The AKC, the UKC, and the United States Dog Agility Association all sponsor agility competitions. Although Boxers are athletic dogs, they are not known for their extreme speed. Therefore, Boxers will participate in agility for fun and training, but they are usually not competitive with faster breeds like Border Collies and Shetland Sheepdogs.

and grooming, walking nicely on the leash, sit, down, stay, and come. Upon the successful completion of all ten exercises, the dog is awarded the title "CGC."

For more information about CGC tests, contact a dog trainer or dog training club in your area.

Photo by Isabelle Francais

Temperament tests evaluate a dog's potential as breeding stock, as a future working dog, or can simply be a way to see how your dog may react in any given situation.

Temperament Test

The American Temperament Test Society was founded to provide breeders and trainers with a means of uniformly evaluating a dog's temperament. By using standardized tests, each dog would be tested in the same manner. The tests can be used to evaluate potential breeding stock, future working dogs, or simply as a way for dog owners to see how their dog might react in any given situation.

For information about temperament tests in your area, contact a local trainer or dog training club.

Therapy Dogs

Dog owners have known for years that our pets are good for us, but now researchers are agreeing that dogs are good medicine. Therapy dogs go to nursing homes, hospitals, and children's centers to provide warmth, affection, and love to the people who need it most. Boxers make great therapy dogs. For more information, contact your local dog trainer to find out about a group in your area.

Schutzhund

Schutzhund is a sport that originated in Germany to evaluate working dogs. Dogs are trained and tested in obedience, tracking, and protection work. Protection work must be approached with a great deal of forethought because teaching a dog to bite is serious and a potential liability. However, when undertaken with good, responsible training, schutzhund is a reputable and legitimate sport for Boxers.

FLYBALL

Flyball is a great sport for dogs that are crazy about tennis balls. This sport consists of a team of four dogs and owners competing against an opposing team of four dogs. The dogs—one from each team at a time—run down the course, jump four hurdles, and then trigger a mechanism that spits out a tennis ball. The dog then turns, jumps the four hurdles again, and returns to his owner. The team that completes the relay first wins. Boxers can run and jump with the best of athletic dogs, but are usually not as fast as Border Collies, Australian Shepherds, or Shetland Sheepdogs, and therefore, aren't usually as competitive. However, flyball is still a fun sport for you and your dog.

Your pet's warmth and affectionate nature can provide comfort and companionship to someone in need. Consider entering your Boxer into a therapy dog program.

Photo by Isabelle Francais

7 Problem PREVENTION and Solving

Photo by Isabelle Francais

Although what you may consider to be problem behavior—barking, digging, chewing—are very natural behaviors to your dog, most can be controlled or prevented.

TRAINING

Training can play a big part in controlling problem behavior. A fair, upbeat, yet firm training program teaches your dog that you are in charge, that he is below you in the family pack, and should reinforce his concept of you as a kind, calm, caring leader. In addition, your training skills give you the ability to teach your dog what is acceptable and what is not.

Boxers are an intelligent breed with a quirky streak to their personality. That quirky streak can be a lot of fun, but it can also get your dog into trouble. Because Boxers are also easily trained, many Boxer owners are flabbergasted when their beloved dog has chewed up the sofa cushion or chased the family cat to the top of the china hutch. Unfortunately, problem behavior can have many causes and solving it isn't always easy.

Many of the behaviors that dog owners consider problems—barking, digging, chewing, jumping up on people, and so on—aren't problems to your Boxer. In fact, they are very natural behaviors to him. Boxers like to jump up on people; that's where the breed's name came from. Dogs dig because the dirt smells good or because there's a gopher in the yard. Dogs bark to verbalize something, just as people talk. All of the things that you consider problem behavior are very natural behaviors to your dog. However, most problem behavior can be worked with and either prevented, controlled, or in some cases, stopped entirely.

WHAT CAN YOU DO?

Health Problems

Some experts feel that 20 percent of all commonly seen behavior problems are caused by health-related problems. A bladder infection or a gastrointestinal upset commonly causes housetraining accidents. Medications can cause behavior changes. Thyroid problems can cause a behavior change, as can hyperactivity, hormone imbalances, and a variety of other health problems.

Photo by Vincent Serbin

Twenty percent of all commonly seen behavior problems are caused by health-related problems. Make an appointment with your veterinarian if your Boxer's behavior changes.

If your dog's behavior changes, make an appointment with your veterinarian. Tell your vet why you are bringing the dog in; don't just ask for an exam. Tell your vet that your Boxer has changed his behavior, explain what the behavior is, and ask if he could look for any physical problems that could lead to that type of behavior.

Don't automatically assume your dog is healthy. If a health problem is causing the behavior change, training or behavior modification won't make it better. Before beginning any training, talk to your veterinarian. Once health problems are ruled out, then you can start working with the problem.

Nutrition

Nutrition can play a part in causing or solving behavior problems. If your dog is eating poor-quality food, or if he cannot digest the food he is being fed, his body may be missing some vital nutrients. If your Boxer is chewing on rocks or wood, chewing the stucco off the side of your house, or grazing on the plants in your garden, he may have a nutritional deficiency of some kind. Some dogs develop a type of hyperactivity when fed a high-calorie, high-fat dog food. Other dogs have food allergies that may show up as behavior problems. If you have any questions about the food your dog is eating, talk to your veterinarian.

Play

Play is different from exercise, although exercise can be play. The key to play is laughter. Researchers know that laughter is wonderful medicine—it makes you feel better—and when you laugh, you feel differently about

Be sure to make time for play—it's a great stress reliever and is necessary for your Boxer's mental health.

Be sure your dog eats foods containing high levels of linoleic acid to help maintain healthy skin and a shiny coat; foods containing high levels of digestible proteins are also desirable. Photo courtesy of Nutro Products, Inc.

the world around you. Laughter and play have a special place in your relationship with your dog. Boxers can be very silly and you should take advantage of that. Laugh at him and with him and play games that will amuse you both. Play is also a great stress reliever; make time for play when you are having a hard time at work. Play with your Boxer after training sessions.

Sometimes dogs get into trouble intentionally because they feel ignored. To these dogs, any attention—even corrections or yelling—is better than no attention at all. If you take time regularly to play with your dog you can avoid some of these situations.

Prevent Problems from Happening

Because many of the things we consider to be problems are natural behaviors to your Boxer, you need to prevent as many of them from happening as you reasonably can. Put the trash cans away so that he never discovers that the kitchen trash can is full of good tasting surprises. Make sure the kids put their toys away so that your Boxer can't chew them to pieces. It's much easier to prevent a problem from happening than it is to break a bad habit later. Preventing mishaps might require that you fence off the garden, build higher shelves in the garage, or perhaps even build a dog run for your Boxer.

Part of preventing problems from occurring also requires that you limit your dog's freedom. A young puppy or untrained dog should never have unsupervised free run of

EXERCISE

Exercise is just as important for your Boxer as it is for you. Exercise works the body, uses up excess energy, relieves stress, and clears the mind. The amount of exercise needed depends upon your dog and your normal routine. A fast-paced walk might be enough for an older Boxer, but a young, healthy Boxer might need a good run or vigorous game of fetch.

A DOG RUN

A dog run is not a dog prison; instead, it is a safe place he can stay while he's unsupervised. The dog run should provide him with protection from the sun and weather, unspillable water, and a few toys. Don't put him in his run as punishment, and never scold him in his run. Instead, give him a treat or a toy when you put him in his run and leave a radio on a quiet, easy listening station in a nearby window.

Photo by Isabelle Francais

You can control your Boxer's unruly behavior by having him sit or lie down.

the house; there is simply too much he can get into. Instead, keep him close to you and close off rooms. If you can't watch him, put him in his run or out in the backyard.

DEALING WITH SPECIFIC PROBLEMS

Jumping on People

Just about every Boxer owner, at one time or another, has to deal with their dog jumping up on people. That's just the way the breed is. And unfortunately, Boxers don't simply jump up, they jump up and wave their front paws around like that proverbial human boxer. Those paws can hurt!

You can, however, control the jumping by emphasizing the sit. If your Boxer is sitting, he can't be jumping up. By teaching him to sit for petting, praise, treats, and meals, you can teach him that the sit is important and that everything he wants will happen only when he sits.

Use the leash as much as you can to teach your Boxer to sit. Solid, muscular dogs, Boxers can be tough to hold on to unless you have something to grab hold of, and the leash is your best training tool. When you come home from work, don't greet your dog until you have a leash and collar in hand. As your dog greets you, slip the leash over his head. Then you can help him sit. If he tries to jump, snap and release the leash and use a verbal correction, "No jump! Sit!" Of course, as with all of your training, praise him when he sits.

When you are out in public, make sure your Boxer sits before any of your neighbors or friends pet him. Again, use your leash. If he won't sit still, don't let anyone pet him—even if you have to explain your actions, "I'm sorry, but I'm trying to teach him manners and he must sit before he gets any petting."

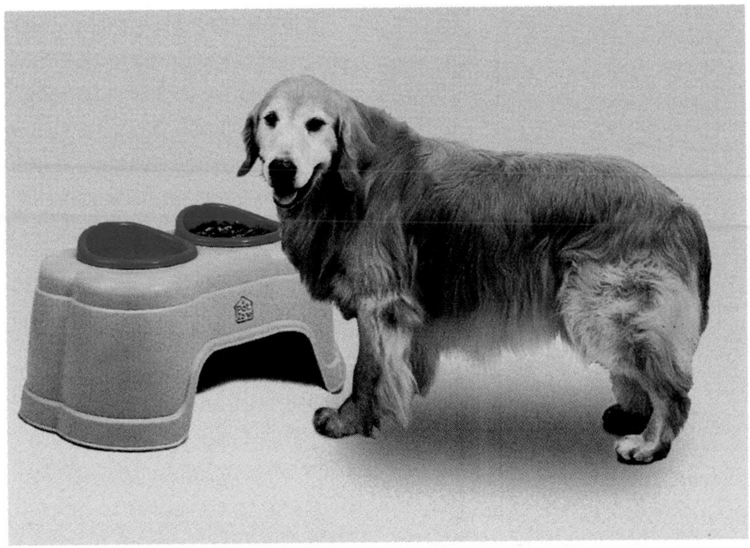

Prevent problems before they start. Veterinarians recommend elevated feeders to help reduce stress on your dog's neck and back muscles. The raised platform also provides better digestion while reducing bloating and gas. Photo courtesy of Pet Zone Products, Ltd.

The key to correcting your dog when he jumps up on people is to make sure the bad behavior is not rewarded. If someone pets your Boxer when he jumps up, that jumping has been rewarded. However, receiving all of the attention when he's sitting will make sitting more attractive to him.

Digging

If your backyard looks like a military artillery range, you need to concentrate first on preventing this problem from occurring. If you come home from work to find new holes in the lawn or garden, don't correct your dog then. He probably dug the holes after you left in the morning and a correction ten hours later won't work.

Instead, build a dog run for him and leave him there during the day. If you fence off one side of your yard next to your house, you might be able to give him a run that is 6 feet wide by 20 feet long. That's a great run. Let him trash this section to his heart's content; that's his yard. Then, when you are home and can supervise him, you can let him have free run of the rest of your yard.

Photo by Isabelle Francais

Your dog may be barking excessively to get attention. If your Boxer is becoming a problem barker, there are a number of techniques that will train him to be quiet.

When he starts to get into trouble, you can use your voice to interrupt him, "Hey! What are you doing? Get out of the garden!"

The destructive dog also needs exercise, training, and playtime every day to use up his energy, stimulate his mind, and allow him to spend time with you. And, don't let this dog watch you garden. If you do, he may come to you later with all of those bulbs you planted earlier in his mouth.

The Barker

Boxers are not normally problem barkers. However, a Boxer left alone for many hours each day may find that barking gets him attention, especially if your neighbors yell at him.

Start teaching him to be quiet when you're at home with him. When your Boxer starts barking, tell him, "Quiet!" When he stops, praise him. When he understands what you want, go for a short walk, leaving him home. Listen, and when you hear him start barking, go back inside and correct him. After a few corrections, when he seems to understand, ask your neighbor to help you. Go outside, stand in front of your house, and ask your neighbor to come out to talk. Have the kids out front playing. When your dog barks because he's feeling left out, go back inside and correct him. Repeat as often as you need to until he understands.

You can reduce your dog's emotional need to bark if you make leaving and coming home a quiet and low-keyed event. When you leave the house, don't give him hugs or tell him repeatedly to be a good dog; that simply makes your leaving more emotional. Instead, give him attention an hour or two prior to leaving, and when it's time for you to go, just go. When you come home, ignore your dog for a few minutes. Then whisper hello to him. Your Boxer's hearing is very good, but to hear your whispers he is going to have to be quiet and still.

You can also distract your dog when you leave. Take a brown paper lunch bag and put a couple of treats in it, maybe a dog biscuit, a piece of carrot, and a slice of apple. Roll the top over to close it and rip a very tiny hole in the side to give your dog encouragement to get the treats. As you walk out the door or gate, hand the bag to your dog. He will be so busy figuring out where the treats are and how to get them, he'll forget you are leaving.

EXTRA HELP

Problem barkers may need extra help, especially if your neighbors are complaining. There are anti-bark collars on the market, and several are very humane and effective. All are triggered by the dog's barking and administer a correction to the dog. Some collars make a high-pitched sound, one squirts a whiff of citronella, and others administer a shock. I do not recommend the shock collars for most Boxers; many will panic at this correction. However, the first two collars are quite effective for many dogs.

Dashing Through Doors and Gates

This is actually one of the easier behavior problems to solve. Teach your Boxer to sit at all doors and gates, then hold that sit until you give him permission to go through or to get up after you have gone through. By teaching him to sit and wait for permission, you will eliminate the problem.

Start with your dog on leash. Walk him up to a door. Have him sit, tell him to stay, and then open the door in front of him. If he dashes through, use the leash to correct him (snap and release) as you give him a verbal correction, "No! Stay!" Take him back to his original position and do it again. When he will hold the sit at this door, go to another door or gate and repeat the training procedure.

When your dog will wait (while on leash) at all doors and gates, take his leash off and hook up his long line. Fasten one end of the long line to a piece of heavy furniture. Walk him up to the door and tell him to sit and stay. Drop the long line to the ground and, with your hands empty, open the door and stand aside. Because your hands are empty (meaning you aren't holding the leash), your Boxer may decide to dash. If he does, the long line will stop him, or you can step on the line. Give him a verbal correction, too, "No! I said stay!" and bring him back to where he started. Repeat the training session here and at all other doors and gates.

Photo by Isabelle Francais

If you have attempted to correct a behavior and still have problems, contact your local dog trainer or behaviorist for some advice.

Other Problems

Many behavior problems can be solved or at least controlled using similar techniques. Try to figure out why your Boxer is doing what he's doing (from his point of view, not yours). What can you do to prevent the problem from happening? What can you do to teach your dog not to do it? Remember, as with all of your training, a correction alone will not change the behavior; you must also teach your dog what you want him to do. If you still have some problems, or if your dog is showing aggressive tendencies, contact your local dog trainer or behaviorist for some help.

RUNNING FREE

If your Boxer does make it out through a door or gate, don't chase him. The more you chase after him, the better the game, as far as he's concerned. Instead, use the shaker from the come command training. Shake it and say, "Do you want a cookie? Come!" When he comes back to you, you must praise him for coming even though you may want to wring his neck for dashing through the door. Don't correct him; a correction will make him avoid you more the next time it happens.

8 Have Some FUN With Your Training

Training has a tendency to be serious; after all, much of training is teaching your Boxer what his place in the family is and how to control himself. That can be serious stuff. However, training can be fun, especially from a Boxer's viewpoint. Teaching your dog games and tricks can challenge your training skills and your Boxer's ability to learn. Once you have taught him, you can have a great time showing off your dog's tricks, amusing your friends, and just plain having fun together.

RETRIEVING

Most Boxers like to retrieve; they just don't always understand the need to bring back what they go out after. However, once you teach your Boxer to bring back the toy, retrieving games can be great fun as well as good exercise.

If your Boxer likes to retrieve, then all you need to do is get him to bring the toy back

If your Boxer refuses to give you the toy he has retrieved, don't play tug-of-war with him. Simply squeeze his muzzle gently until he lets go.

Photo by Isabelle Francais

to you. When you throw the toy and he goes after it, wait until he picks it up. Once he has it in his mouth, call him back to you with a happy tone of voice. If he drops the toy, send him back to it. If he brings the toy all the way back to you, praise him enthusiastically.

Don't let him play tug-of-war with the toy. If he grabs it and doesn't want to let go, reach over the top of his muzzle and tell him "Give," as you press his top lips against his teeth. You don't have to use much pressure, just enough so that he opens his mouth to relieve the pressure. When he gives you the toy, praise him. If your Boxer likes to take the toy and run with it, have him drag his long line behind him while he plays. Then, when he dashes off, you can step on the line and stop him. Once you've stopped him, call him back to you.

The name game is a great way to make your Boxer think. With practice, he'll learn to identify his toys by name.

THE NAME GAME

The name game is a great way to make your dog think. And don't doubt him for a minute; your Boxer can think. When you teach your dog the names of a variety of things around the house, you can put him to work, too. Tell him to pick up your keys or your purse, or send him after the remote control to the television. The possibilities are unlimited.

Start with two items that are very different, perhaps a tennis ball and a magazine. Sit on the floor with your Boxer and place the two items in front of you. Ask him, "Where's the ball?" and bounce the ball so that he tries to grab it or at least pays attention to it. When he touches it, praise him and give him a treat.

Once he is responding to the ball, lay it on the floor and send him after it. Praise and reward him. Now set several different items out with the magazine and ball and send him after the ball again. After he is doing well, start all over again with one of his other toys. When he will get his toy, put the toy and ball out on the floor together and send him after one or the other. Don't correct him if he makes a mistake, just take the toy away from him and try it again. Remember, he's learning a foreign language (yours) at the same time that he's trying to figure out what the game is, so be patient.

THE COME GAME FOR PUPPIES

Two family members can sit on the ground (or floor) across the yard or down the hallway from each other. Each should have some treats for the puppy. One family member can call the puppy from across the yard (or down the hall) and when the puppy reaches her, she should praise the puppy and give him a treat. She can then turn the puppy around so that he's facing the other family member who can call the puppy. This very simple game can make teaching the come command exciting for the puppy. In addition, kids can play this game with the puppy, giving them a chance to participate in the puppy's training.

FIND IT

When the dog can identify a few items by name, you can start hiding those items so that he can search for them. For example, once he knows the word "keys," you can drop your keys on the floor under an end table. Tell your Boxer, "Find my keys!" and help him look, "Where are they?" and move him toward the table. When he finds them, praise him enthusiastically.

As he gets better, make the game more challenging. Make him search in more than one room. Have the item hiding in plain sight or underneath something else. In the beginning, help him, and always help him when he appears confused. But don't let him give up; make sure he succeeds.

HIDE AND SEEK

Start by having a family member pet your Boxer, offer him a treat, and then send him away to another room. Tell your Boxer, "Find Dad!" and let him go. If he runs right to Dad, praise him. Have different family members play the game so that he can search for each of them and learn their names.

As he gets better at the game, the family member hiding will no longer have to pet the

Photo by Isabelle Francais

Hide and seek is a fun game for the whole family. While playing, encourage your Boxer to use his nose and scenting abilities to succeed.

dog at the beginning of the game; he can simply go hide. Help your dog initially so that he can succeed at the game, but encourage him, too, to use his nose and his scenting abilities.

SHAKE HANDS

Shaking hands is a very easy trick to teach. Have your dog sit in front of you. Reach behind one front paw and as you say, "Shake!" tickle his leg in the hollow just behind his paw. When he lifts his paw, shake it gently and praise him. When he starts lifting his paw on his own, stop tickling.

WAVE

When your dog is shaking hands reliably, tell him "Shake. Wave!" and instead of shaking his paw, reach toward it without taking it. Let him touch his paw to your hand, but pull your hand away so that he's waving. Praise him. Eventually, you want him to lift his paw higher than for the shake and to move it up and down so he looks like he's waving. You can do that with the movements

HAVE FUN WITH TRICKS

I taught one of my dogs, Michi, to play dead and we both had a lot of fun with it. Michi got so good at it that he could pick the phrase "dead dog" out of casual conversation. One day, Michi and I were out front congratulating the son of a neighbor of mine who had just graduated from the police academy and was proudly wearing his new uniform. As I shook the police officer's hand, I turned to Michi and asked him, "Would you rather be a cop or a dead dog?" Michi dropped to the ground, went flat on his side, and closed his eyes. The only thing giving him away—that he was really just having fun—was the wagging tail! Meanwhile, my neighbor's son was stuttering and turning red. He didn't know if he should be offended or if he should laugh. It was great fun.

Photo by Isabelle Francais

Trick training is limited only by your imagination and your ability to teach your dog. This Boxer puppy could charm anyone with just a wave of his paw.

of your hand as he reaches for it. Praise him enthusiastically when he does it right. When he understands the wave, you can stop your hand movements.

ROLL OVER

With your Boxer lying down, take a treat and make a circle with your hand around his nose as you tell him, "Roll over." Use the treat (in the circular motion) to lead his head in the direction you want him to roll. Your other hand may have to help him. Boxers have a big rib cage, and it may take some effort on your dog's part to start the roll-over movement.

MAKE UP YOUR OWN TRICKS

What would you and your Boxer have fun doing? Teach him to stand up on his back legs and dance. Teach him to jump through a hula hoop or to jump through your arms as they form a circle. Teach him to play dead or to sneeze. Trick training is limited only by your imagination and your ability to teach your dog.

SUGGESTED READING

BOOKS BY T.F.H. PUBLICATIONS

JG-117
A New Owner's Guide to Dog Training
Dorman Pantfoeder
160 pages, over 100 full-color photos

TS-258
Training Your Dog for Sports and Other Activities
Charlotte Schwartz
160 pages, 170 full-color photos

TS-273
The World of the Boxer
Richard Tomita
496 pages, 800 full-color photos

JG-109
Training the Perfect Puppy
Andrew DePrisco
160 pages, over 200 full-color photos